Living LITERATURE

CONTEXTS

Susan Cockcroft

Hodder & Stoughton

A MEMBER OF THE HODDER HEADLINE GROUP

Acknowledgements:

The authors and publishers would like to thank the following for their kind permission to reproduce copyright material:

p10 *Cross* by Lanston Hughes, published by Serpents Tail. Reproduced by permission of David Higham Associates; p11 *Queen Kong* by Carol Ann Duffy, reproduced with permission of Macmillan, London, UK; p13 an extract from *Wind* by Ted Hughes from *The Hawk in the Rain*. Reproduced with permission of Faber and Faber Ltd; an extract from *The Tale of Tom Kitten* by Beatrix Potter © Frederick Warne & Co., 1906, 2002. Reproduced by kind permission of Frederick Warne & Co. p14 an extract from *1984* by George Orwell © George Orwell, 1949. Reproduced by kind permission of Bill Hamilton as the Literary Executor of the Estate of the Late Sonia Brownell Orwell and Martin Secker & Warburg Ltd; p14 an extract from *Sula* by Toni Morrison, published by Chatto & Windus. Used by permission of The Random House Group Limited; p15 an extract from *Cat on a Hot Tin Roof* by Tennessee Williams. *Cat on a Hot Tin Roof* © 1954, 55 renewed 1982, 83 The University of the South. Published through special arrangement with The University of the South, Sewanee, Tennessee; p18 an extract from *Gentlemen Prefer Blondes* by Anita Loos The International Magazine Co., Inc. (Harper's Bazaar), 1925 © Anita Loos, 1925. Copyright assigned to Anita Loos Trust, 1984. All rights reserved; p18 an extract from 'Her Last Chance' in *Talking Heads* by Alan Bennett reproduced with the permission of BBC Worldwide Limited © Alan Bennett 1988; p19 an extract from *The Wasteland* by T.S. Eliot. Reproduced with permission of Faber and Faber Ltd; p19 an extract from *The Lost Continent* by Bill Bryson, 1989 © Bill Bryson, published by BlackSwan, a division of Transworld Publishers; p20 *Mrs Beast* by Carol Ann Duffy, reproduced with permission of Macmillan, London, UK; p23 an extract from *Harry Potter and the Philosopher's Stone* by JK Rowling © JK Rowling 1998; p13 and 24 and extracts from *Down Under* by Bill Bryson © Bill Bryson, published by Black Swan, a division of Transworld Publishers. All rights reserved; p24 an extract from *An Inspector Calls* by J.B. Priestly © J.B. Priestly 1947, by permission of PFD on behalf of the Estate of J.B. Priestly; p25 an extract from *Death of an Expert Witness* by P.D. James. Reproduced by permission of Faber and Faber Ltd; p25 an extract from *White Teeth* by Zadie Smith (Hamish Hamilton, 2000 © Zadie Smith 2000); p26 *Slough* by John Betjeman from *Collected Poems,* reproduced by permission of John Murray (Publishers) Ltd; p29 an extract from *Lady Chatterley's Lover* by D.H. Lawrence, 1928. Reproduced by permission of Pollinger Limited and the Estate of Frieda Lawrence Ravagli; pp32–33 an extract from *Love in a Cold Climate* by Nancy Mitford (Penguin, 1954) © Nancy Mitford 1954, 1949; p33 *The Belfry* by R.S. Thomas © R.S. Thomas, published by Weidenfeld & Nicolson. Used by permission of Orion Publishing Group Ltd; pp34–35 an extract from *Life isn't all ha ha hee hee* by Meera Syal, published by Doubleday. Used by permission of Transworld Publishers, a division of The Random House Group Limited; pp35–36 an extract from *Angela's Ashes* by Frank McCourt, 1997. Reprinted by permission of HarperCollins Publishers Ltd © Frank McCourt 1997; p43 an extract from Mrs Dalloway by Virginia Woolf, reproduced by permission of the Society of Authors as the literary representatives of the estate of Virginia Woolf; p44 an extract from *The Wasteland* from *Collected Poems 1909–1962* by T.S. Eliot, reproduced by permission of Faber and Faber Ltd; p44 an extract from *The Sound and the Fury* by William Faulkner. Reproduced with permission of Curtis Brown Group Ltd, London on behalf of Random House Inc. © William Faulkner 1931; p45 an extract from *The Portrait of the Artist as a Young Girl* edited by John Quinn. Reproduced by permission of The Random House Group Ltd. p46 a range of quotations from *The Agony and the Ego* by C. Boylan (ed.); p51 *The General* by Siegfred Sassoon © Siegfried Sassoon by kind permission of George Sassoon; p51 *Skin-teeth* from *I is a Long Memoried Woman* by Grace Nichols © 1983/2002 Karnak House; pp53–54 *My Father's Father's Father* from *Carrying my Wife* by Moniza Alvi, Bloodaxe Books, 2000. Used by kind permission of Bloodaxe Books; pp54–55 *Waiting Gentlewoman* from *Selected Poems* by U.A. Fanthorpe, 1986 from *Standing To*, reproduced by permission of Peterloo Poets; p55 an extract from *Nice Work* by David Lodge, 1988, published by Martin, Secker and Warburg, reprinted by permission of the Random House Group Ltd; pp81–82 an extract from an article in *The Guardian* by Simon Hoggart © *The Guardian,* 13/12/01; pp99–100 an extract from *Hugh Selwyn Mauberley* from *Collected Shorter Poems* by Ezra Pound. Used by permission of Faber and Faber Ltd; p101 *Musee des Beaux Arts* from *Collected Poems* by W.H. Auden, 1940. Used by permission of Faber and Faber Ltd; pp102–103 *Green Amber in Riga (for Gunnar Cirulis)* from *Forward Book of Poetry* by Sujata Bhatt, 2001. Used by kind permission of Carcanet Press Limited; p104 *Piccadilly Line* from *Selected Poems* by Carole Satyamurti, Bloodaxe Books, 2000. Used by kind permission of Bloodaxe Books; pp105–106 an extract from *At the Bay* by Katherine Mansfield, 1922, reproduced by kind permission of Orion Children's Books; p107 an extract from *Invisible Man* by Ralph Ellison, 1952, Random House Inc.; pp108–109 *A History of the World in 10½ Chapters* by Julian Barnes, 1989; an extract from *What's bred in the bone* by Robertson Davis, Penguin, 1987 © Robertson Davis 1985; p112 an extract from *Long Day's Journey into Night* by Eugene O'Neill, published by Jonathon Cape. Reprinted by permission of The Random House Group Limited; pp113–114 an extract from *The Caretaker* by Harold Pinter, 1960, reproduced with permission of Faber and Faber Ltd; p115 an extract from *Cloud Nine* by Caryl Churchill © 1979, 1980, 1983, 1984, 1985 by Caryl Churchill. Reproduced by permission of Nick Hern Books, www.nickhernbooks.co.uk; pp117–118 an extract from *A Short Walk in the Hindu Kush* by Eric Newby, 1958.

Every effort has been made to trace copyright holders of material reproduced in this book. Any rights not acknowledged will be acknowledged in subsequent printings if notice is given to the publisher.

Orders: please contact Bookpoint Ltd, 130 Milton Park, Abingdon, Oxon OX14 4SB. Telephone: (44) 01235 827720, Fax: (44) 01235 400454. Lines are open from 9.00 – 6.00, Monday to Saturday, with a 24 hour message answering service. Email address: orders@bookpoint.co.uk

British Library Cataloguing in Publication Data
A catalogue record for this title is available from The British Library

ISBN 0 340 799536

First published 2000
Impression number   10 9 8 7 6 5 4 3 2 1
Year   2007 2006 2005 2004 2003 2002

Copyright © 2002 Susan Cockcroft

Cover photo from Association Chaplin © 2002 Ray Export Company Establishment.
Typeset by Fakenham Photosetting Limited, Fakenham, Norfolk NR21 8NN.
Printed in Great Britain for Hodder & Stoughton Educational, a division of Hodder Headline Plc, 338 Euston Road, London NW1 3BH by Martins the Printers, Berwick upon Tweed.

Contents

Introduction

Our aim in this book is to investigate **context** as it relates to **literature**. But what does the actual word 'context' mean? It's used today in a wide variety of situations, from politics and business to gossip between friends on the phone. Look at the following examples:

a In the context of world-wide recession it was decided to forgo staff bonuses this Christmas.
b 'Why was she wearing that crazy outfit at college today?' 'Oh – well the context is that someone bet her twenty quid she wouldn't wear her mum's 60s outfit all day.' 'Oh, that explains it! I thought she'd totally lost the plot!'
c The lecturer's comments on his history essay made better sense in the context of the handout he'd missed.

Here is a basic definition of *context*: the extra information not immediately or obviously available, making it possible for someone not 'in the know' to understand an unpredictable, confusing or mystifying situation. *Chambers Dictionary* (1998) defines *context* as 'the parts of a piece of writing or speech which precede and follow a particular word or passage and *may fix, or help to fix, its true meaning* [our italics]'. Another definition is 'associated surroundings, setting'.

We can get some more help if we look at the etymology (word history) of *context*. It comes from the Latin preposition *con* ('with') added to the participial verb form *textum* ('woven'). Literally, *context* means 'with woven' or (more elegantly) 'woven together'. Notice too that the familiar word *text* comes from a similar source: mediaeval Latin *textus,* 'text' derives from *textus* ('structure') which also derives from *textum*.

When we refer to a *text*, A Level English students tend to think of a set book. In the media today, the term *text* can refer to a film or an advertisement just as easily as to written or scripted language. However, for the purposes of this book on literature and context, the idea of *text* as a 'woven structure' is more useful to us. 'Weaving' *literally* means crossing threads or strands of material to produce cloth; *metaphorically* it suggests 'constructing, fabricating, producing, contriving' something. So we can reasonably describe a *text* as a 'woven structure of words, sound patterns, grammar, syntax and imagery'. Concealed within its fabric (to continue the metaphor!) are the strands of extra information *which make up the context of the text*. The aim of this book is to enable you as readers to discover new meanings within texts by examining their contexts.

Chapter 1 explores the idea of context in relation to the *writer* and *reader* of a text, after briefly looking at how context has become central to the

A Level Specifications for English Literature and English Language and Literature. After more detailed exploration of the concept of *text*, we introduce the ideas of *reading and writing positions* in relation to texts.

Chapter 2 involves a more detailed consideration of ***context from a readerly position***, in which we explore the ways in which people read texts both as *individuals* and as *members of society*. We shall see how readers *interact* with texts as they read them, and how these different *interactive* readings can actually change the context of a text.

Chapter 3 focuses on ***context from a writerly position***, whether the position is as an *individual* or as a *representative of society*. This will lead to a brief investigation of the whole creative process of writing, within the framework of context. Finally we shall establish a methodology for investigating context in texts, to be applied in the next three chapters.

In **Chapters 4, 5** and **6** *context* will be explored in relation to a wide variety of texts from different historical periods, by a range of writers and in a variety of genres, both literary and non-literary. Each chapter focuses on texts written within a specific time period (though not necessarily of the same length of time) for two reasons. Firstly, this should help you to link *genre* with literary *history* and literary *context*, and secondly, it will introduce you to some exciting and unusual texts. The structure of each chapter is the same: after a broad-ranging introduction to the period, and a timeline, there will be four sections, focusing on *poetry, literary prose, drama* and *non-literary prose*. At the end of each individual section there will be an opportunity for you to practice your newly acquired skills of contextual analysis on an unseen text.

Chapter 4 focuses on the period from Chaucer to the late seventeenth century, and looks at comedy, tragedy, love poetry, a pamphlet and a diary. **Chapter 5** applies the investigative model to poetic satire, the novel, melodrama and travel writing, from the early eighteenth century to the end of the nineteenth century. **Chapter 6** focuses on the twentieth and the early twenty-first centuries, and investigates some varied examples of the new and experimental in literature, from the short story and absurdist drama to experimental prose, before drawing the book to a conclusion.

1 Unpicking Context

Part 1: What is Context?

Context in spoken language

In spoken language (i.e. casual conversation), knowing the *context* can make all the difference. If somebody makes a reference we don't recognise, whether it's with friends and family or in a less familiar environment, we need to know the *context* of what they're talking about in order to respond appropriately and avoid putting our foot in it. In conversation you can sometimes pick up verbal and non-verbal clues to help establish the *context* (especially necessary if you're slightly embarrassed to ask *what* or *who* is being discussed). Long practice in social relations means that as soon as we have even *partly* identified the context, we're at ease and ready to join in the conversation.

ACTIVITY 1

Look at the following list of utterances and quotations. Your task is to suggest different and appropriate *contexts* for each one.

1. 'What on earth are we going to do now? I was so sure they'd catch the train.'
2. 'May the words of my mouth and the meditations of all our hearts . . .'
3. 'Can you tell me what the trouble is?'
4. 'Can I help?'
5. 'It is the East and Juliet is the sun.'
6. 'Just pop off your jacket, would you?'
7. 'Too many cooks spoil the broth.'
8. 'Have a nice day!'
9. 'How may I help you?'
10. 'Candidates are reminded that . . .'

Context in written language

In written language it's not so easy. Presented with a passage from a *non-literary text* (e.g. advertising, textbook, instruction manual, newspaper article etc.) we can usually recognise the genre and often the audience and purpose as well ('Isn't this is an ad for that new face-cream that's supposed to prevent spots as well as moisturise? Look at all that scientific guff – they're trying to blind us with science and then persuade us to spend ten pounds for a single tube!'). But with *literary texts* we are more uncertain, though all A Level English students should comfortably manage the basic differences between prose, poetry and drama (varying line-lengths for the first two and layout of dialogue for the third). Beyond these simple genre differences, we tend to have problems. Request information about the approximate date (or even *century*) of a literary text; ask for a description of typical generic features; ask about who the author might be, or for some information about the times they lived in – and many people who enjoy and regard themselves as knowledgeable about literature may find themselves coming unstuck. (This doesn't apply to English teachers!)

ACTIVITY 2

Below is a list of 10 short extracts from a range of literary and non-literary texts. You have also been given a list of 10 genres.

a Match the passages with the genres/ audiences.

b Identify the approximate date (century would do!) of each extract *and* its primary purpose (i.e. persuade, inform, entertain, instruct).

Genres: children's story   personal letter   broadsheet article   play lyric poem   fiction   advertising leaflet   nursery rhyme   news report instructional writing

Extracts

1 The Tory leadership contest descended into ferocious civil war yesterday.

2 The earth's surface is a jigsaw of tectonic plates, each a slab of rock hundreds of kilometres across. Pressure builds up in the fault lines between these plates, and when a section of rock slips suddenly the result is an earthquake. It appears to be a purely physical process, so it is surprising to discover there is an electrical dimension.

3 When to her lute Corinna sings,
Her voice revives the leaden strings . . .

4 We make a big variety of practical pots for the kitchen and also some plant pots. We have one range in honey-coloured, plain stoneware and another in green with more elaborate decoration.

5 There was an old woman tossed up in a basket
   Seventeen times as high as the moon;
And where she was going, I couldn't but ask it,
   For in her hand she carried a broom . . .

6 I attempted to rise, but was not able to stir: for as I happened to lie upon my back, I found my arms and legs were strongly fastened on each side to the ground; and my hair, which was long and thick, tied down in the same manner. I likewise felt several slender ligatures across my body, from my armpits to my thighs.

7 *PANE CASERECCIO Rustic Pugliese Bread* Nothing is thrown away in an Italian kitchen. Housewives often create works of art with leftovers! *Pane casereccio* is made using all sorts of leftovers of cheese and meat which are still good to eat but too tough to slice. You can use any type of hard cheese, from grated Parmesan to pecorino, provolone or scamorza.

8 *Algernon* Yes, but this isn't your cigarette case. This cigarette case is a present from someone of the name of Cecily, and you said you didn't know anyone of that name.

Jack Well, if you want to know, Cecily happens to be my aunt.
Algernon Your aunt!
Jack Yes. Charming old lady she is, too. Lives at Tunbridge Wells. Just give it back to me, Algy.
Algernon [*retreating to back of sofa*] But why does she call herself Cecily if she is your aunt and lives at Tunbridge Wells? [*reading*] 'From little Cecily with fondest love.'

9   The weather grew colder. Silver Lake was frozen. Snow fell, but always the wind blew the ice clean, drifting the snow into the tall grass of the sloughs and driving it into waves on the low shores. On the whole white prairie nothing moved but blowing snow, and the only sound in the vast silence was the sound of the wind.

10 *24 February* Pardon the liberty I now take in addressing you, I am not sure whether it is a prudent action or not, neither do I care; woman has but a narrow path to walk upon but she will sometimes do things she ought not when self-defence and honour are connected in the case. The reason I take this step is this, I should like you to justify your past conduct towards me.

The purpose of this activity was to focus your attention on *written* language; to remind you about the existence of *non-literary* as well as *literary* genres; and to start to demonstrate the importance of understanding the context of a written text. But before we go any further, let's confirm the **centrality of context** to all A Level Literature and A Level Language and Literature Specifications by reminding ourselves of the Assessment Objectives:

AS Literature candidates are required to 'show understanding of the *context* in which literary texts are written and understood';
A2 Literature candidates have to 'evaluate the significance of cultural, historical and other *contextual* influences';
AS and A2 Language and Literature candidates must 'evaluate the significance of cultural, historical and other *contextual* influences on literary texts and study'.

ACTIVITY 3

Activity 2 provided you with an opportunity to match texts (however fragmented) with contextual information about them (however limited). Your decisions were probably a mixture of knowledge and guesswork. Activity 3 is designed to provide you with 'hands on' experience in investigating the *context* of a literary text of your own choice.

a   Choose a literary text. It can be familiar or unfamiliar, and in any literary genre – but it should have some interest and appeal for you.

b   Find out as much as possible about the **context** of your text and make brief notes.

c   Give a short presentation (5 minutes *maximum*) about its context to your group.

Likely sources of information include books like the *Oxford Companion to English Literature*, any encyclopaedia (*Pears*), relevant literary criticism or biography and the Internet (try search engines like Altavista and Google). The following questions may help you to structure your presentation.

1 *What does the book itself tell you?* (e.g. author, title, date of publication, place of publication; length; physical appearance; use of illustrations)
2 *What can you deduce about genre, purpose and audience?* (don't worry if these all blur together a little)
3 *What can you find out about the author?* (brief but *relevant* details)
4 *What were the big political and social events when this text was written?* (again, very brief notes to get the *feel* of the period)

5 *What did people think of your text when it was first published?* (you might find an early review if your text has an introduction)
6 *What do critics think of it now?* (look at the blurb on the back, or again, try the introduction for a contemporary opinion)
7 *What do you think about this text?* (if you don't know it already, read the first chapter/first scene/a few poems to get some sense of what it's about – and jot down your reactions!)

Don't go over the top with your information-gathering – it's only a short presentation! You may want to discuss afterwards which presentation was most interesting and helpful about context, and why.

Context: the writer and the reader(s)

The questions listed above were intended to help you to establish the context of a particular literary text within the framework of an activity. If you now look more closely at the questions, you will see that the first four are about *the way the text was produced by its author*, within his or her social and historical environment. In other words, these questions establish a text's **context of writing**. The last three questions focus on what people *thought about a text when it was first published, and what they think today –* in other words, the history of its publication and reception. (Remember that these critical opinions or *readings* may well be influenced by whatever was/is intellectually fashionable at the time.) Add to this the opinion of the *individual* reader (whose response comes as a product of his or her life experience), and you have the **context of reading** of any given text. Let's look at these in more detail.

Context of writing

Who are the writers of texts? The obvious answer is – all of us. Not only are we experienced *readers* of texts, but we are also *writers* of texts from childhood onwards. Many people of all ages enjoy creative writing, and experiment with stories, plays or poems or script writing. Whatever we – as individuals – write, has its own **context of writing**, influencing *what* we write about and *how* we write. Contributory factors to this *context of writing* may include some or all of the following: gender, age, class, education, family, ethnicity, work experience or occupation, friendship groups, culture, religion and ideology etc. Our individual response to the public issues of the day may be part of this *context of writing*, and we may also be influenced (knowingly or otherwise) by current public cultural and political attitudes and assumptions. Again, these will be part of the *context of writing*.

ACTIVITY 4

a Find a piece of your own creative writing (recent or written some time ago). Write down as much as you can remember about its *context of writing*. (You may find the previous paragraph helpful here.) For example, who gave you the initial idea for the text? Was it a teacher's suggestion, or your own idea? Do you remember how easy/difficult it was to write? How did you feel about it then and what do you think about it now? Did anyone else read it – what was their reaction?

b When you have completed your own *context of writing*, compare the notes you made with other people's in your group. Some will remember that they wrote as a class exercise, others may remember an event (public or private) which made them put pen to paper; others may recall an emotional experience which triggered his or her writing. The point to note is that effective writing tends to come from a strong sense of personal involvement – and this is a key part of the *context of writing*.

ACTIVITY 5

The following activity involves a comparison between two texts produced by two different writers (a poet and a diarist) on the same topic. The first text is a poem by the nineteenth-century Romantic writer, William Wordsworth; the second is an extract from his sister Dorothy Wordsworth's *Journal*. The brother and sister lived in Grasmere in the Lake District, where Dorothy acted as housekeeper, diarist and devoted supporter to her brother up to and after his marriage. In this poem Wordsworth recalls a past event to show how poetry *recreates emotion*, thus conveniently providing us with a clear example of this poem's *context of writing*.

Read both texts through carefully and then answer the following questions:

a List the physical details *common to both texts*.
b What details in Dorothy's journal does William *not* include?
c What additional points does Wordsworth make in his poem about the daffodils and their effect on him and on his imagination?
d How important would you think sharing this experience was for the poet?
e Do you think that other readers would benefit from knowing the poem's *context of writing*?

I Wandered Lonely as a Cloud

I wandered lonely as a cloud
That floats on high o'er vales and hills,
When all at once I saw a crowd,
A host of golden daffodils;
Beside the lake, beneath the trees,
Fluttering and dancing in the breeze.

Continuous as the stars that shine
And twinkle on the milky way,
They stretched in never-ending line
Along the margin of a bay:
Ten thousand saw I at a glance,
Tossing their heads in sprightly dance.

The waves beside them danced; but they
Out-did the sparkling waves with glee:
A poet could not be but gay,
In such a jocund company:
I gazed – and gazed – but little thought
What wealth the show to me had brought.

For oft, when on my couch I lie
In vacant or in pensive mood,
They flash upon that inward eye
Which is the bliss of solitude;
And then my heart with pleasure fills,
And dances with the daffodils.

Glossary: jocund means 'joyful', 'happy'

William Wordsworth (1804)

We set off after dinner … The wind was furious … [it] seized our breath the Lake was rough. … When we were in the woods beyond Gowbarrow park we saw a few daffodils close to the water side. We fancied that the lake had floated the seeds ashore and that the little colony had so sprung up. But as we went along there were more and yet more and at last under the boughs of the trees, we saw that there was a long belt of them along the shore … I never saw daffodils so beautiful they grew among the mossy stones about and about them, some rested their heads on these stones as on a pillow for weariness and the rest tossed and reeled and danced and seemed as if they verily laughed with the wind that blew upon them over the lake, they looked so gay ever glancing ever changing.

Dorothy Wordsworth's *Journal* (April 15 1802)

Context of reading

Reading a text seems to be a perfectly straightforward activity, but – once we've conquered the mechanics – is it the same kind of experience for everyone? First of all there's the basic difference between 'reading for pleasure' and reading as a task, which we all recognise (the difference between an English 'set text' and the *Harry Potter* series or *The Lord of the Rings*). Reading as individuals means that we choose what we want to read and that our responses to a large extent will be governed by our personal experience: an old man, for example, will read *King Lear* rather differently from a teenage girl. Hence as *individuals* our **context of reading** is determined by our life experience, knowledge and attitudes. Furthermore, these will differ not only for every individual reader, but they will also differ depending on the historical period in which that reader lived or lives.

For example, because our literacy rate is so high, many people today can read a Shakespeare text without too much difficulty. In contrast, many ordinary Elizabethans were illiterate, and could not have read *Hamlet* even if a text (rather than just an acting script) had been available. Nevertheless the Elizabethan audience would not have experienced our problems with Shakespeare's text, because our *context of reading* is so different from theirs. (*Watching* a performance is a different matter – we can make sense of this, just as the sixteenth-century Elizabethan audience did.) Another example of social and political change over time affecting the *context of reading* for the twentieth- or twenty-first-century reader is Jonathan Swift's *Gulliver's Travels* (1726). Intended as a biting political satire on eighteenth-century life, many readers today would describe it as a children's book!

Another sort of individual reading is *reading as a critic*, which is a different version of reading as an individual (see above). The critic starts from the same reading position as everyone else – until he or she is invited to express a professional opinion. A literary critic's task is to inform, explain and persuade the audience/readership of a particular point of view by offering *a reading or interpretation* of a literary text. Of course, a single text can produce a range of critical interpretations, which may be highly subjective, or influenced by critical fashion, or deliberately subversive. These varied interpretations are *also* part of the context of reading. The twentieth century has seen many developments in literary critical theory, some deriving from politics (Marxist and new historicist criticism), some from psychology (Freudian or psychoanalytic criticism), some from linguistics (structuralism, deconstruction), some from social science (feminist criticism) and some from multi-culturalism (post-colonial criticism). We shall offer some brief definitions of each below. What is important is that these new ways of interpreting literary texts have in all cases extended the **context of reading** for whichever text is under consideration.

Reading as a critic: some critical approaches

a Reading from a psychoanalytic perspective

This approach derives from the work of Freud and Jung, and their theories about the human psyche, its structure and drives. For our purposes it is a way of reading which draws attention to the psycho-sexual aspects of character and relationships, focuses on the sense of self (and self-alienation), and explores the unconscious as well as the conscious mind. Characteristic literary strategies include symbolism and 'stream of consciousness' narrative methods.

b Reading from Marxist and new historicist perspectives

These approaches are basically similar, in that they view texts from social and historical perspectives. For example, Marxist critics see literary texts as *products* of their society and of its economic and political ideologies. Issues of power and powerlessness are central to Marxist as well as to new historicist criticism, especially the way in which texts can be *subversive*. Characteristic literary features include realism and the differing languages (discourses) of power.

c Reading from a post-structuralist perspective

This approach derives in part from linguistics, especially the idea of language as a structured sign system (words have assigned meanings, just like the colours of traffic lights). As a way of critical reading, structuralists and post-structuralists look at the form and organisation of texts, at the way contrasts and tensions exist (*binary oppositions*), at the 'centres of interest' in a text, and at what's left on the margins. Deconstructionist critics take post-structuralism even further, and are especially interested in the gaps, absences and 'holes' in a text – what's left unsaid. For example, we can read *Jane Eyre* both from the structuralist and deconstructionist positions. A *structuralist* reading might emphasise the *binary oppositions* (e.g. man/woman; employer/employee; freedom/restriction or imprisonment). A *deconstructionist* reading, on the other hand, might focus on the gaps and silences – Bertha Rochester's story, Mrs Fairfax and Grace Poole's collusion.

d Reading from a feminist perspective

Interpreting a text from a feminist perspective can mean 'reading as a woman' (whatever one's gender); it can also mean exploring the way women are *represented* and *represent themselves* within a text, perhaps focusing on power relations or the use of gender stereotypes.

e Reading from a post-colonial perspective

In the twentieth century much important literature in English has been produced in the former British colonies such as India, Australia, New Zealand, parts of Africa, Canada, the West Indies and America – although distinctly American literature had been appearing since the mid-seventeenth century. This 'external' colonisation (cf Robert Pope, *The English Studies Book*, page 138) has been balanced by 'internal' colonisation of Scottish, Welsh and Irish literature in English. If you read texts from a post-colonial perspective you have to be aware of the *different Englishes*; of representations of multi-cultural societies; of the dangers of misreading from a Western or strictly British English perspective; of ethnic and racial stereotyping and of marginalising. Although this sounds hard to do, it can be summed up succinctly – make no assumptions, read carefully and be extra open-minded. Indeed, this is true of all these *ways of reading*; they are meant to enlarge the **context of reading**, not close it down and make it rigid.

ACTIVITY 6

Try out your skills as interpreters of texts by attempting the following task.
Produce a short (one paragraph) critical reading of each of the following nursery rhymes from the perspective indicated. Compare your three readings with those of other people in your group.

Jack and Jill (feminist reading)
Little Miss Muffet (psychoanalytic reading)
Baa Baa Black Sheep (Marxist reading)

Putting it into practice: identifying the contexts of writing and reading in literary texts

We shall now turn to some 'real' texts so that you can practice your skills in identifying the *context of writing* and the *context of reading*.

ACTIVITY 7

Some introductory information is provided about each text and its author as *context*. The idea is that you 'match up' the information provided with the subject matter of the text. This will enable you to make brief notes on the *contexts of writing and reading* for each extract. (Don't worry though if there's more to say on the one than the other.) To make it quite clear, we'll start with a worked example.

Worked Example

Wilfred Owen fought in the trenches in World War 1, was invalided out with shell shock, but returned to the front to be killed a week before the war ended. His poetry reflects the horror of his experiences and his anger at the suffering of his fellow soldiers.

Dulce et Decorum Est (October 1917–March 1918)

Bent double, like old beggars under sacks,
Knock-kneed, coughing like hags, we cursed through sludge,
Till on the haunting flares we turned our backs
And towards our distant rest began to trudge.
Men marched asleep. Many had lost their boots
But limped on, bloodshod. All went lame; all blind;
Drunk with fatigue; deaf even to the hoots
Of tired, out-stripped Five-Nines that dropped behind.

Gas! Gas! Quick, boys! – An ecstasy of fumbling,
Fitting the clumsy helmets just in time;
But someone still was yelling out and stumbling
And flound'ring like a man in fire or lime ...
Dim, through the misty panes and thick green light,
As under a green sea, I watched him drowning ...

COMMENTARY

Context of writing: knowing that Owen fought in the trenches in World War 1 gives this poem a sense of immediacy as we note the evidence of his personal involvement ('we cursed', 'I watched') and his detailed knowledge of the terrible effects of gas attacks ('coughing like hags') on the retreating soldiers who 'limped on, bloodshod'.

Context of reading: the effect on the reader of this horrific description is powerful, exercising the imagination to the full. Owen intends this, and as we read the extract, our fear and hatred of war increases ('I watched him drowning').

TEXT 1

Charles Dickens wrote the novel *Bleak House* (1852–3) in mid-career. A journalist as well as a fiction writer, Dickens had a strongly developed social conscience, and in this book aimed to raise public awareness of the sufferings of the poor and the indifference of the rich and powerful. The narrator is Esther Summerson, the saintly but appealing young heroine.

I was glad when we came to the brickmaker's house; though it was one of a cluster of wretched hovels in a brickfield, with pigsties close to the broken windows, and miserable little gardens before the doors, growing nothing but stagnant pools. Here and there, an old tub was put to catch the droppings of rain-water from a roof, or they were banked up with mud into a little pond like a large dirt-pie. At the doors and windows, some men and women lounged or prowled about, and took little notice of us except to laugh to one another, or to say something as we passed, about gentlefolks minding their own business, and not troubling their heads and muddying their shoes with coming to look after other people's.

TEXT 2

Langston Hughes (1902–1967) was an influential black American writer who was a key figure in the Harlem Renaissance of the 1920s. Born in the South, he was educated in the North (including Columbia University in New York) and travelled widely, working as a sailor and earning a precarious living in Paris before returning to New York. As a poet he was much influenced by jazz and the Blues.

Cross

My old man's a white old man
And my old mother's black
If ever I cursed my white old man
I take my curses back.

If ever I cursed my black old mother
And wished she were in hell,
I'm sorry for that evil wish
And now I wish her well.

My old man died in a fine big house.
My ma died in a shack.
I wonder where I'm gonna die,
Being neither white nor black?

TEXT 3

The following extract is part of a love poem written by John Donne (who later became Dean of St Paul's Cathedral in London) to his mistress. Published in the collection *Songs and Sonets* (1633), it was probably written in the 1590s. The poem contains references to voyages of exploration and to the founding of the American colonies.

The Goodmorrow

And now good morrow to our waking souls,
   Which watch not one another out of fear;
For love, all love of other sights controls,
   And makes one little room an everywhere.
   Let sea-discoverers to new worlds have gone.
   Let maps to others, worlds on worlds have shown,
Let us possess one world, each hath one and is one.

TEXT 4

Carol Ann Duffy, in her collection *The World's Wife* (1999), imagines from a feminist perspective what it might have been like to be married to some of the famous men of the past. In this following poem the fantasy is extended to famous figures of film history, and she imagines what it would have been like to be King Kong's wife, Queen Kong.

Queen Kong

I remember peeping in at his skyscraper room
and seeing him fast asleep. My little man.
I'd been in Manhattan a week,
making my plans; staying at 2 quiet hotels
in the Village, where people were used to strangers
and more or less left you alone ...

He'd arrived, my man, with a documentary team
to make a film ...
... I found him alone
in a clearing, scooped him up in my palm,
and held his wriggling, shouting life till he calmed.
For me, it was absolutely love at first sight.

Part 2: What is a Text?

We have explored the meanings of *context*, and differentiated between the *context of writing* and the *context of reading*. Let's look now at what we actually mean by the term *text*. Throughout the book, we shall be using it to describe examples of a wide range of genres, from literary (poetry, drama and fiction) to non-literary (travel literature, diaries, speeches, letters, biography etc.). It's worth noting that the word is used today to refer not only to examples of written and spoken forms, but also to visual media like film, television and advertising. Definitions of the word can be simple: '... text is any instance of a verbal record' (Pope page 234) or complex: 'Text is linguistic communication (either spoken or written) seen simply as a message coded in its auditory or visual medium' (J. Hawthorn (1994) *Concise Glossary of Contemporary Linguistic Theory* page 213).

We shall avoid both versions, and go for our own working definition:

> *Text is spoken or written language which communicates a message in a particular way which we can either see or hear.*

A brief history of the text

The next question is – why have we become so *text-oriented*? The reason for this is part of the history of twentieth-century critical thought. Literary criticism became an academic discipline in its own right in this century (you can take undergraduate courses in Critical Theory now). As we have already seen (page 7) new ways of *reading* texts emerged, and people began to investigate the whole process of literary creation more closely. Some critics in the 1940s refused to look at anything other than the poetic text itself (New Critics), considering the poet and the audience irrelevant. You could analyse the anatomy and inner workings of the poem – but you mustn't stray beyond these boundaries!

Then a new influence on literary criticism emerged – linguistics. All of a sudden, a poetic text was not a corpse to be dissected, but a living act of communication between poet and reader – both vital to its existence. (Indeed most critics would argue that a text doesn't *have* any existence unless it has been read or heard by someone.) This author–text–reader relationship is shown below in a simple diagram. Notice that there are alternative terms for each key word, and that the entire process works *in both directions*.

Figure 1

Author ←→	Text ←→	Reader
sender	message	receiver
addressor	message	addressee

Does *context* have any place in this diagram of human verbal communication? Since we explored the *context of writing* and the *context of reading* earlier, it shouldn't be difficult to see where each fits into the diagram. There is, however, a new feature to note – namely that a text has its own *context*, which means the *code* or language choice or style of the individual text itself. A revised version of the diagram looks like this:

Figure 2

Author ←→ *context of writing*	Text ←→ *context of text*	Reader *context of reading*
sender	message	receiver
addressor	message	addressee
	Code	

ACTIVITY 8

The purpose of this activity is to demonstrate the importance of choosing the right *code* in a variety of situations involving spoken and written language. Your task is to select, from the following list, the right *code* for the appropriate situation. (People who are poor communicators are always choosing the wrong *code* for the situation and audience, and offending everyone!) NB the same code may be used *more than once*.

Situation	Code
visiting grandparents	jargon
review of local concert for NME	casual conversation
job interview	politically correct language
letter of apology to friend for damaging her car	taboo and slang language
evening with friends	formal register
business meeting	politeness strategies
Blind Date contestant	specialised vocabulary
General Studies essay on Victorian sanitation	rhetorical language
political speech	joke telling

ACTIVITY 9

Look at the *code* used by the writers of the extracts below. Your tasks are **a** to identify the genre, purpose and audience and **b** to describe the *code* of each text.

TEXT 1

At some undetermined point in the great immensity of its past – perhaps 45,000 years ago, perhaps 60,000 – but certainly before there were modern humans in the Americas or Europe – it was quietly invaded by a deeply inscrutable people, the Aborigines, who have no clearly evident racial or linguistic kinship to their neighbours in the region, and whose presence in Australia can be explained only by positing that they invented and mastered ocean-going craft at least 30,000 years in advance of anyone else in order to undertake an exodus, then forgot or abandoned nearly all that they had learned and scarcely bothered with the open sea again.

TEXT 2

This house has been far out at sea all night
The woods crashing through darkness, the booming
    hills,
Winds stampeding the fields under the window
Floundering black astride and blinding wet

Till day rose; then under an orange sky
The hills had new places, and wind wielded
Blade-light, luminous and emerald,
Flexing like a mad eye.

TEXT 3

Once upon a time there were three little kittens and their names were Mittens, Tom Kitten and Moppet. They had dear little fur coats of their own; and they tumbled about the doorstep and played in the dust.

Part 3: Texts, Contexts and Audiences

We started this chapter by investigating the idea of context, and looking at differences between the *context of writing* and the *context of reading*. Having established these parameters, we moved towards a better understanding of the concept of *text* by setting up some basic definitions. We looked at the history of text, and linked it with the theory of communication. Before moving on to the final section of the chapter, which concerns relationships between texts (*intertextuality*), it seems a good moment to pause and review where we've got to. The next activity is focused on a range of extracts from different historic periods, all of which are taken from the opening/early stages of the selected genres. The reason for this focus is that the beginning of a poem or novel or play is when the author has to engage the interest of the audience most vigorously and establish a dynamic communication. How does he or she do this? By creating appealing characters, offering intriguing description, creating emotional tension or suspense, amusing, shocking or surprising us – there are almost infinite possibilities. One thing the writer must do, however, is to establish some kind of *context* for whatever is going to take place.

ACTIVITY 10

Read the following extracts carefully. In each extract the writer's purpose is to communicate something important to the reader. This might be mood, theme, situation, relationship, character – it depends! Your task is to answer the following questions about each extract:

a What is the literary genre of the extract? On what evidence do you base this?

b How does the writer establish mood and atmosphere? Give brief examples.

c What is the *context* for the extract?

TEXT 1: *Worked Example*

It was a bright cold day in April, and the clocks were striking thirteen. Winston Smith, his chin nuzzled into his breast to escape the vile wind, slipped quickly through the doors entering along with him.

George Orwell *1984* (1949)

We can deduce that this is a relatively modern text (Winston is probably wearing a modern overcoat; there are 'doors' suggesting a modern entrance; his name itself conjures the mid-twentieth-century political figure, Winston Churchill; 'vile' is Twenties/Thirties slang). However, the one jarring note is the fact that *all* the clocks were 'striking thirteen' i.e. not just one faulty one! We are in a world which seems normal but is not – the dystopian world of 1984.

TEXT 2

When my mother died I was very young,
And my father sold me while yet my tongue
Could scarcely cry "'weep! 'weep! 'weep! 'weep!"
So your chimneys I sweep & in soot I sleep ...

William Blake 'The Chimney Sweeper' (1794)
from *Songs of Innocence and Experience*

TEXT 3

In that place, where they tore the nightshade and blackberry patches from their roots to make room for the Medallion City Golf Course, there was once a neighbourhood. It stood in the hills above the valley town of Medallion, and spread all the way to the river. It is called the suburbs now, but when black people lived there it was called the Bottom.

Toni Morrison *Sula* (1973)

TEXT 4

Margaret:	One of those no-neck monsters hit me with a hot buttered biscuit so I have t'change.
Brick:	Wha'd you say, Maggie? Water was on s'loud I couldn't hearya . . .
Margaret:	Well, I! – just remarked that!- one of th' no-neck monsters messed up m' lovely lace dress so I got t'- cha-a-ange . . .
Brick:	Why d' ya call Gooper's kiddies no-neck monsters?
Margaret:	Because they've got no necks! Isn't that a good enough reason?
Brick:	Don't they have any necks?
Margaret:	None visible. Their fat little heads are set on their fat little bodies without a bit of connection.
Brick:	That's too bad.
Margaret:	Yes, it's too bad because you can't wring their necks if they've got no necks to wring! Isn't that right, honey? . . . Yep, they're no-neck monsters, all no-neck people are monsters . . . (*Children shriek downstairs*) Hear them? hear them screaming? I don't know where their voice-boxes are located since they don't have necks. I tell you I got so nervous at that table tonight I thought I would throw back my head and utter a scream you could hear across the Arkansas border an' parts of Louisiana and Tennessee.

Tennessee Williams *Cat on a Hot Tin Roof* (1955)

Part 4: Texts, Contexts and Positions

When we use the word 'position' in conversation, we mean a particular place or location (literal or metaphorical). It might be a seat at the football stadium, a preferred place in class, the spot where something happened, a move in chess or empathising with a friend (putting ourselves in their *place*). So how can this word have anything to do with texts? *Position* in relation to texts refers to 'the place where the writer or reader is coming from' – that is, his or her starting place.

What is the *writerly position*? It means the writer's *place* within his or her life experience and his or her world (i.e. personal history, education and experience; and social, political and cultural milieu). The text is produced or written from this *position*. For example, Dickens wrote several novels (*Great Expectations, Oliver Twist, David Copperfield*) which were narrated from the *position* of a vulnerable small boy attempting to make sense of his world – feelings experienced by Dickens at various low points in his own childhood when family fortunes were low.

In contrast the *readerly position* is where we come from when we read a text. The reading position of an African-American woman reading Toni Morrison's *Beloved* would be different from a European woman with little understanding of black American history, who could empathise but would need much more knowledge before she could read the text from the African-American *reading position.* Our understanding, as readers, of any text will be enhanced by our capacity to *situate* ourselves in an appropriate reading position. For example, if we read *Pamela,* an eighteenth-century epistolary novel (written in letters), with no knowledge of contemporary social practices and attitudes (i.e. the relationship between servants and masters, or attitudes to women), we can hardly complain if it makes little sense.

The *reading position* adopted by literary critics is different again. Their aim is to offer a convincing interpretation of its meaning, sometimes based on subjective opinion, sometimes following a particular theoretical approach (e.g. Marxist, deconstructionist, feminist). On occasion a critic will challenge a well-established interpretation by offering an *oppositional reading* from a radically different position. For example, an oppositional reading of *Macbeth* might present Macbeth himself as the guiltless victim of a plot engineered by the witches and Lady Macbeth (the fourth witch). One of the most famous (and longstanding) oppositional readings is Satan as hero of *Paradise Lost* by John Milton.

ACTIVITY 11

The following activity gives you a chance to investigate the *position* of the poet, John Milton, when he *wrote* the sonnet below. News had just reached England about the massacre of a Protestant sect in Northern Italy in April 1655. Read the biographical (private) and historical (public) information either before or after you read the poem, as you prefer.

Your task is to find *textual evidence* in the poem of Milton's *writing position* (e.g. look at his choice of vocabulary, use of poetic voice and so on).

On the Late Massacre in Piedmont

Avenge, O Lord, thy slaughtered saints, whose bones
   Lie scattered on the Alpine mountains cold;
   Even them who kept thy truth so pure of old
   When all our fathers worshipped stocks and stones,
Forget not: in thy book record their groans
   Who were thy sheep and in their ancient fold
   Slain by the bloody Piemontese that rolled
   Mother with infant down the rocks. Their moans
The vales redoubled to the hills, and they
   To heaven. Their martyred blood and ashes sow
   O'er all the Italian fields, where still doth sway
The triple tyrant: that from these may grow
   A hundredfold, who having learnt thy way
   Early may fly the Babylonian foe.

Biographical information

A distinguished scholar, poet and radical thinker, John Milton (1608–1674) published pamphlets against the church establishment and in defence of the execution of Charles I. He wrote in favour of a free press and of divorce on grounds of incompatibilty. He was Latin Secretary to

Oliver Cromwell, Lord Protector of England after the Civil War. In May 1655 a protest about the massacre was made by Oliver Cromwell which Milton composed.

Historical information

On 24 April 1655 the Waldensians (a Protestant group who had been granted freedom of worship) were slaughtered by the troops of the Catholic Duke of Savoy (probably with the knowledge of the Pope), in their isolated mountain valley in Piedmont in Northern Italy. The excuse was that they had settled in territory forbidden to them. One of their central beliefs was that God should not be worshipped in idols made of wood ('stocks') or stone, in the tradition of primitive Christianity. The 'book' refers to God's record of human conduct which will be used by Him on the Day of Judgement. The Papal mitre (head-dress) consisted of three crowns; the ancient city of Babylon is described in the Bible (Revelations) as a place of sin and corruption; at this period, Protestants regarded Rome as Babylon, and referred to the Pope as the scarlet woman of Babylon.

ACTIVITY 12

In this activity you will have the opportunity to explore the meaning of *reading position* in relation to three texts (extracts). Each text is fictional, and each tells us about the world in which the heroine lives. Texts 1 and 2 are over 100 years apart, Texts 2 and 3 about 60 years apart.

When readers encounter a text, they read (at least partially) in the light of their own gender experience. Their *reading position* (whether they are aware of it or not) is gendered. Your task is to read each text carefully and then answer the following questions. In your answers you should focus on the representation of *character, social values* and *language choice* in each extract, and give brief quotations.

a What would a male reader think about this text at the time it was written?
b What would a male reader think about this text today?
c What would a female reader think about this text at the time it was written?
d What would a female reader think about this text today?

TEXT 1

Emma Woodhouse, handsome, clever, and rich, with a comfortable home and happy disposition, seemed to unite some of the best blessings of existence; and had lived nearly twenty-one years in the world with very little to distress her.

She was the youngest of the two daughters of a most affectionate indulgent father, and had, in consequence of her sister's marriage, been mistress of his house from a very early period. Her mother had died ... long ago ... and her place had been supplied by an excellent woman as governess ... the mildness of her temper had hardly allowed her to impose any restraint ... the shadow of authority being now long passed away, they had been living together as friend and friend very mutually attached, and Emma doing just what she liked; highly esteeming Miss Taylor's judgment, but directed chiefly by her own.

Jane Austen Emma (1816)

TEXT 2

March 20

Mr Eisman gets in tomorrow to be here in time for my birthday. So I thought it would be really delightful to have at least one good time before Mr. Eisman got in, so last evening I had some literary gentlemen in to spend the evening because Mr Eisman likes me to have literary people in and out of the apartment. I mean he is quite anxious for a girl to improve her mind and his greatest interest in me is because I always seem to want to to improve my mind and not waste any time. And Mr Eisman likes me to have what the French people call a "salon" which means that people all get together in the evening and improve their minds ... so we all got together and I called up Gloria and Dorothy and the gentlemen brought their own liquor. So of course the place was a wreck in the morning and Lulu and I worked like proverbial dogs to get it cleaned up, but Heaven knows how long it will take to get the chandelier fixed.

March 22

Well my birthday has come and gone but it was really quite depressing. I mean it seems to me that a gentleman who has a friendly interest in educating a girl like Gus Eisman, would want her to have the biggest square cut diamond in New York. I mean I must say I was quite disappointed when he came to the apartment with a little thing you could hardly see. So I told him it was quite cute, but I had quite a headache and I had better stay in a dark room all day and I told him I would see him the next day, perhaps ... But he came in at dinner time with really a very beautiful bracelet of square cut diamonds so I was quite cheered up.

Anita Loos Gentlemen Prefer Blondes (1926)

TEXT 3

... That is something I pride myself on, actually: I am professional to my finger-tips.

Whatever it is I'm doing, even if it's just a walk-on, I must must must get involved, right up to the hilt. I can't help it. People who know me tell me I'm a very serious person, only it's funny, I never get to do serious parts. The parts I get offered tend to be fun-loving girls who take life as it comes and aren't afraid of a good time should the opportunity arise-type-thing. I'd call them vivacious if that didn't carry overtones of the outdoor life. In a nutshell I play the kind of girl who's very much at home on a bar stool and who seldom has to light her own cigarette ...

Alan Bennett 'Her Last Chance' in Talking Heads (1988)

Part 5: Texts, Contexts and Intertextuality

We have looked at *contexts*, at *texts*, and at *reading* and *writing positions* in relation to texts. Our final task in this chapter is to explore the way *texts relate to* **each other**. (This is a further aspect of context.) In Part 2 of this chapter (page 11–13) we established that a 'text' is part of a dynamic process of communication between author and reader. However, links are often made between texts, and this linking is called **intertextuality**. Who makes these links? It may be the reader who notices connections, picks up allusions (sometimes unintentional on the writer's part); or it may be the writer who deliberately alludes or refers to other texts to achieve a particular purpose. In either case, the use of *intertextual reference* enriches in some way the communication of meaning. Three examples should make it clearer, one from literature, one from film, one using references to both. Since Alfred Hitchcock's *Psycho*, every shower sequence has the potential for terrifying audiences again, and many film-directors have made use of this intertextual reference for their own purposes. In literature, T.S. Eliot is a master of intertextuality (though on occasion his references can be too obscure and alienate the reader). In the following example, however, he succeeds admirably. It's taken from the second poem in Eliot's ground-breaking sequence, *The Waste Land* (1925), in which he details the moral and spiritual corruption of society after the tragedy of World War 1. The poem presents a chilling portrait of women's falseness and betrayal of love.

Eliot's text

The Chair she sat in, like a burnished throne,
Glowed on the marble, where the glass
Held up by standards wrought with fruited vines
From which a golden Cupidon peeped out . . .

'A Game of Chess' from *The Waste Land* (1925)

Intertextual reference

The barge she sat in, like a burnished throne,
Burn'd on the water: the poop was beaten gold;
Purple the sails, and so perfumed that
The winds were lovesick with them;

Shakespeare, *Antony and Cleopatra* (Act II Sc.2)

Intertextuality is used by Eliot to demonstrate the difference between the great love story of the past and the banality of sexual passion in the present. Cleopatra's throne has turned into a chair, and desire is represented by light only ('glowed') – the heat of passion ('burned') has gone. This example of intertextuality works and enriches Eliot's poem because the story of Antony and Cleopatra is well known.

Another example of *intertextuality* mixes types of text references. In Bill Bryson's account of his nostalgic trip round America, *The Lost Continent* (1989), he pays a visit to Mount Rushmore, in California, where the giant heads of former U.S. Presidents are carved out of the mountainside.

Afterwards I drove to Mount Rushmore, a couple of miles outside town up a steep road. I had always wanted to see Mount Rushmore, especially after watching Cary Grant clamber over Thomas Jefferson's nose in *North by Northwest* (a film that also left me with a strange urge to strafe someone in a cornfield from a low-flying aeroplane). . . . The monument looked smaller than I expected. . . . In fact, Mount Rushmore is enormous. Washington's face is sixty feet high, his eyes eleven feet wide.

The film *North by Northwest* stars Cary Grant as hero. In the final scenes he is pursued all over the precipitous carved monument by the villains, having already avoided being machine-gunned by a crop-spraying light aeroplane. The intertextual references are uncomplicated: the humour lies in the contrast between Grant the hero and Bryson the tourist.

The following poem by Carol Ann Duffy is actually constructed by *intertextual reference*. The first example is the title *Mrs Beast*. If you think 'fairytale', you should rapidly pick up the reference to the story of Beauty and the Beast. Your task is to unpick the rest of the intertextual references (they've been set in italics to help you), and to explain how they work in the poem.

Mrs Beast

These myths going round, these legends, fairytales
I'll put them straight; so when you stare
into my face – *Helen's* face, *Cleopatra's,*
Queen of Sheba's, Juliet's – then deeper
gaze into my eyes – *Nefertiti's, Mona Lisa's,*
Garbo's eyes – think again. *The Little Mermaid* slit
her shining, silver tail in two, rubbed salt
into that stinking wound, got up and walked,
in agony, in fishnet tights, stood up and smiled, waltzed,
all for a Prince, a pretty boy, a charming one
who'd dump her in the end, chuck her, throw her overboard.
I could have told her – look love, I should know,
they're bastards when they're Princes.
What you want to do is find yourself a Beast.

Summary

In this chapter we started with a working definition of *context*, and then moved to a brief exploration of the *context of reading* and the *context of writing*. Next we looked at the concept of *text* in terms of dynamic process and at reading and writing *positions*. Finally we looked at the use of *intertextuality* as part of the framework of context.

2 Context from the Reader's Perspective

I t would not be unreasonable to wonder why this second chapter is focusing on context from the position of the *reader* rather than the *writer*. We have already spent some time looking at the *author–text–reader* dynamic, so why not follow its logic and start with the *writer*? Firstly, there are many more readers than writers of the sorts of texts we are discussing; secondly, readers influence writers greatly by their known expectations of a text (e.g. romantic fiction writers know just what their readers expect in terms of their hero and heroine); and thirdly, the *author–text–reader dynamic* works in *both* directions as a continuous process of communication. If we can reach a good understanding of 'the reader' we are well on our way to understanding context from the reader's perspective. But before proceeding, we shall take a minute to consider an important aspect of critical theory not discussed in the first chapter (because it fits better here), *reader-response theory*. You should rest assured that you will not be expected to *apply* it – however, you should certainly have some basic familiarity with it, simply because without theoreticians like Stanley Fish and Harold Bloom the significance of *readers* in the interpretation of texts would still be unrecognised.

A simplified account of reader-response theory

- There is more than one *reader* of a text.
- The *implied reader* means the reading audience the author expected; it can also mean the audience the text 'created' itself (because readers *responded* to it).
- The *inscribed reader* means the reader who 'fits' the text and who is comfortably at home with it.
- The *intended reader* is whoever the author says he or she wrote for.
- The *ideal reader* means the reader who will extract maximum value from a particular text.
- The *informed reader* is every writer's dream – he or she knows the language of the created text, understands its range of meanings as well as the relevant literary conventions.
- The *empirical reader* means the person capable of reading texts in a variety of ways.

Can we look at a text in the light of these ideas about *reader-response*? We shall try them out on *Jane Eyre* by Charlotte Brontë, a text which remains a bestseller over 150 years after its publication in 1847. Firstly, the novel undoubtedly appealed to an unexpectedly wide audience (not just to women, her *implied readers*). Her *inscribed readership* would include conventional and less conventional women, because both could warm to the seemingly conventional but actually rebellious heroine. Brontë's *ideal reader* would certainly be sympathetic to her presentation of the trials of an educated but impoverished woman in nineteenth-century society. The *informed readership* whose enthusiastic interest led to *Jane Eyre's* runaway success were probably educated women and liberal men. Today we are all *empirical readers* because extensive social change has enabled us to read earlier texts from a range of perspectives.

Part 1: Making a Start: From Theory to Practice

We shall now go back to basics and leave theory on hold, to be referred to as and when required. There are four questions to be addressed in relation to the idea of 'the reader'. *Who is the reader? What does he or she read? Why do people read? How do they read?*

Who is the reader?

'Know thyself' was apparently written in the temple at Delphi in Greece, where the famous Oracle could be consulted. Our self-knowledge increases as we mature and experience more of the world, learning through our interaction with others and through the way we deal with different challenges. One way to discover a little more about ourselves as *readers* is by noting down exactly what books we most enjoy.

ACTIVITY 14

a Make a list of the last ten books you read which you *enjoyed*; it doesn't matter how far back you have to go – children's books count too. (You may be interested to record which genres you preferred.)

b Ask a friend or member of your family to write down five words or phrases which describe you well (e.g. *adventurous, witty, quiet, short-tempered*).

c Exchange book lists and character descriptions with another member of your group (preferably someone who knows you well). Compare the lists – does the book list reflect the character description, or are there any surprises?

d Discuss in your group whether people think that personal preference in books *does* tell us about someone's personality/character.

What do we read?

Having completed the previous activity, we have some incidental evidence about what a particular group of students has read. We could even have produced our own survey of the group's reading preferences overall (perhaps divided into genres). Another way to find out what people read is to look at the list of bestselling books published weekly (hardback/softback, fiction/non-fiction). You can also look on the shelves at major bookshops.

Why do we read?

This is a harder question to answer: the obvious response is that certain books fulfil our needs as readers. But why do we have these strong preferences? Although it may seem a little simplistic, perhaps preferences in books are linked with personality and character, as we implied previously in Activity 14. For example, someone might prefer the *detective story genre* because they enjoy solving puzzles, experiencing tension, fear, even horror; someone else might opt for *romantic fiction* or *adventure* or *travel writing* motivated by different kinds of escapism. Reading *autobiography* and *biography* satisfies a desire for information (together with the slightly gossipy pleasure of knowing the 'inside' story), as well as the opportunity to experience life vicariously! Again, we read books or comics for the pleasure of laughing – but also, perhaps, motivated by escapism. Why do we read *poetry*? Probably to see the world differently, to fire the imagination, to enjoy the musicality of language and again, perhaps, to escape ordinary existence. The genres of *science fiction* (utopias and dystopias) and *fantasy* exercise the imagination, and enable us to have a different slant on 'reality'. And we could go on – but the point has been made. What we read depends very much on who we are and what is happening to us.

ACTIVITY 15

The following extracts have been taken from bestselling texts in a range of genres. Working with a partner, choose three or four texts which interest you. Your task is:

a to identify the *genre* and *audience*
b to suggest *reasons* for its bestselling status
c to report your findings back to the group.

In answering **b** you may find it helpful to look at: *topic, language choice, presentation of character, tone, use of dialogue, figurative language, sound patterning, appropriacy to audience.* (You will find a list identifying the extracts at the end of the chapter.)

TEXT 1

Professor Binns paused again, pursing his lips, looking like a wrinkled old tortoise. 'Reliable historical sources tell us this much,' he said, 'but these honest facts have been obscured by the fanciful legend of the Chamber of Secrets. The story goes that Slytherin had built a hidden chamber in the castle, of which the other founders knew nothing. Slytherin, according to the legend, sealed the Chamber of Secrets so that none would be able to open it until his own true heir arrived at the school. The heir alone would be able to unseal the Chamber of Secrets, unleash the horror within, and use it to purge the school of all who were unworthy to study magic.'

There was silence as he finished telling the story, but it wasn't the usual sleepy silence that filled Professor Binns's classes. There was unease in the air as everyone continued to watch him, hoping for more. Professor Binns looked faintly annoyed.

'The whole thing is arrant nonsense, of course,' he said.

TEXT 2

Flying into Australia, I realized with a sigh that I had forgotten again who their Prime Minister is . . . But then Australia is such a difficult country to keep track of. On my first visit, some years ago, I passed the time on the long flight from London reading a history of Australian politics in the twentieth century, wherein I encountered the startling fact that in 1967 the Prime Minister, Harold Holt, was strolling along a beach in Victoria when he plunged into the surf and vanished. No trace of the poor man was ever seen again. This seemed doubly astounding to me – first that Australia could just *lose* a Prime Minister (I mean, come on) and second that news of this had never reached me.

TEXT 3

Inspector (taking charge, masterfully): Stop!

They are suddenly quiet, staring at him.

And be quiet for a moment and listen to me. I don't need to know any more. Neither do you. The girl killed herself – and died a horrible death. But each of you helped to kill her. Remember that. Never forget it. (*He looks from one to the other of them carefully.*) But then I don't think you ever will. Remember what you did, Mrs Birling. You turned her away when she most needed help. You refused her even the pitiable little bit of organized charity you had in your power to grant her. Remember what you did –

Eric (unhappily): My God – I'm not likely to forget.

Inspector: Just used her for the end of a stupid drunken evening, as if she was an animal, a thing, not a person. No, you won't forget. (*He looks at Sheila.*)

Sheila: I know. I had her turned out of a job. I started it.

Inspector: You helped – but didn't start it. (*Rather savagely, to Birling*) You started it. She wanted twenty five shillings a week instead of twenty two and sixpence. You made her pay a heavy price for that. And now she'll make you pay a heavier price still.

Birling (unhappily): Look, Inspector – I'd give thousands – yes, thousands –

Inspector: You're offering money at the wrong time, Mr. Birling. (*He makes a move as if concluding the session . . .*) No, I don't think any of you will forget.

TEXT 4

Now it so happened that Mr Pickwick and his three companions had resolved to make Rochester their first halting-place too; and having intimated to their new-found acquaintance that they were journeying to the same city, they agreed to occupy the seat at the back of the coach, where they could all sit together.

'Up with you,' said the stranger, assisting Mr Pickwick on to the roof with so much precipitation as to impair the gravity of that gentleman's deportment very materially.

'Any luggage, sir?' inquired the coachman.

'Who – I? Brown paper parcel here, that's all, – other luggage gone by water . . .

'Heads, heads – take care of your heads!' . . . as they came out under the low archway

... 'Terrible place – dangerous work – other day – five children – mother – tall lady, eating sandwiches – forgot the arch – crash – knock – children look round – mother's head off – sandwich in her hand – no mouth to put it in – head of a family off – shocking, shocking!'

TEXT 5

The call had come at six-twelve precisely. It was second nature to him now to note the time by the illuminated dial of his electric bedside clock before he had switched on his lamp, a second after he had felt for and silenced the raucous insistence of the telephone. It seldom had to ring more than once, but every time he dreaded that the peal might have woken Nell. The caller was familiar, the summons expected. It was Detective Inspector Doyle. The voice, with its softly intimidating suggestion of Irish burr, came to him strong and confident, as if Doyle's great bulk loomed over the bed.

'Doc Kerrison?' The interrogation was surely unnecessary. Who else in this half-empty, echoing house would be answering at six-twelve in the morning? He made no reply and the voice went on.

'We've got a body. On the wasteland – a clunch field – a mile north-east of Muddington. A girl. Strangulation by the look of it. It's probably pretty straightforward but it's as close ...'

'All right, I'll come.'

TEXT 6

Early in the morning, late in the century, Cricklewood Broadway. At 6.27 hours on 1 January 1975, Alfred Archibald Jones was dressed in corduroy and sat in a fume-filled Cavalier Musketeer Estate face down on the steering wheel, hoping the judgement would not be too heavy upon him.

... though he did not know it, and despite the Hoover tube that lay on the passenger seat pumping from the exhaust pipe into his lungs, luck was with him that morning. The thinnest covering of luck was on him like fresh dew. Whilst he slipped in and out of consciousness, the position of the planets, the music of the spheres, the flap of a tiger moth's diaphanous wings in Central Africa, and a whole bunch of other stuff that Makes Shit Happen had decided it was second-chance time for Archie. Somewhere, somehow, by somebody, it had been decided that he would live.

TEXT 7

   O what to her shall be the end
And what to me remains of good?
   To her, perpetual maidenhood,
And unto me no second friend.

Dark house, by which once more I stand
   Here in the long unlovely street,
   Doors, where my heart was used to beat
So quickly, waiting for a hand,

A hand that can be clasped no more –
   Behold me, for I cannot sleep,
   And like a guilty thing I creep
At earliest morning to the door.

He is not here; but far away
   The noise of life begins again,
   And ghastly through the drizzling rain
On the bald street breaks the blank day ...

TEXT 8

Come, friendly bombs, and fall on Slough
It isn't fit for humans now,
There isn't grass to graze a cow
    Swarm over, Death!

Come, bombs, and blow to smithereens
Those air-conditioned, bright canteens,
Tinned fruit, tinned meat, tinned milk, tinned beans
    Tinned minds, tinned breath.

Mess up the mess they call a town –
A house for ninety-seven down
And once a week a half-a-crown
    For twenty years,

And get that man with double chin
Who'll always cheat and always win,
Who washes his repulsive skin
    In women's tears,

And smash his desk of polished oak
And smash his hands so used to stroke
And stop his boring dirty joke
    And make him yell.

But spare the bald young clerks who add
The profits of the stinking cad;
It's not their fault that they are mad,
    They've tasted hell . . .

Come, friendly bombs, and fall on Slough
To get it ready for the plough.
The cabbages are coming now:
    The earth exhales.

How do we read?

The last question – *how* we read – is probably something you haven't thought about much since you were five or six. A more focused version of the same question would be – how do you **interact** with texts?

Reading silently in whatever situation we find ourselves in (at home, when travelling etc) is completely familiar, yet even there people read and react differently. There's the individual who suddenly laughs out loud in a silent Tube carriage; the easily distracted reader in the dentist's waiting room; the furiously concentrated reader (the cliche 'avid reader' seems to fit) in the library; or the teenager lost in a magazine (oblivious to requests for help with the washing-up).

Reading aloud is different – some people love it (enjoying the sound of their own voices), whereas others detest being asked to do it. The *context* is often a classroom, if the request is formal – reading aloud to friends from a magazine or a letter is different, and usually not a problem. The most extreme version of 'reading aloud' is usually some kind of performance where the reader adds his or her own *interpretation* of the text – a further layer of meaning. Of course, when the text is a play, the next move is to *performance*; 'reading' is simply the first stage towards the actor's interpretation.

Two more aspects of our interaction with texts are pace and level of commitment. Most of us are quite happy to describe ourselves as fast or slow readers. Both descriptions have negative and positive connotations. Fast readers notoriously skip as they rush through the book – but they revel in the stimulus and excitement of the narrative. Slow readers, on the other hand, enjoy the subtleties of the narrative – but get bogged down by detail and can (literally) lose the plot. Most of us are a little bit of both; unfortunately studying texts for assessment purposes tends to require more of the latter!

How committed a reader are you? Do you remember as a child reading the cornflakes packet or the jam label rather than having *nothing* to read? Some people read sporadically, enjoying one book and then not reading for a while. Others are miserable if they haven't always got a book 'on the go'. Most of us recognise the special pleasure of having a particularly good book to read, which we become almost reluctant to finish. There is almost a cline of reading commitment, from the laid-back, casual approach (I can pick it up or put it down – whatever) to the passionate reader (traditionally called a bookworm) who is only happy with a book in the hand. (A Level students tend to position themselves towards the middle of this cline or continuum.)

ACTIVITY 16

This is a simple on-going activity which may interest you if you have contact with young children (baby-sitting etc.) or have access to a local primary school. The aim is to note the way young children respond to hearing stories *read aloud*. How easy is it to engage and retain their attention? Do you think watching television has changed the way children respond to being read to? Compare notes with members of your group.

Part 2: Looking at Context from the Reader's Position

Addressing these questions makes us more aware of the process of reading, and the needs of readers. It is out of our personal situation/context that we make decisions about what and when we read, and it is within the *context* of our lives that the reasons for our reading choices are located. Bearing this in mind, we shall move into the main area of focus in this chapter, starting with an important distinction. As readers of literature, we read within two basic contexts; the context of *individual private experience* and the context of *social or public experience*.

An extreme example of the impact of public and private experience would be linked with the two World Wars. Although very few men and women remain alive today who remember the horrors of World War 1, many more survive who lived through World War 2, and experienced at first hand prisoner-of-war or concentration camps. For them, such memories are ineradicable (whether spoken about or not). They have lived the rest of their lives within the dual contexts of traumatic individual and social experiences. In this case the links between public and private experience are virtually seamless, because of the all-pervasive nature of war.

In most other situations, public events – however significant – have less generalised impact on individuals, making it possible to differentiate much more clearly between the *context of individual experience* and the *context of social experience.*

Reading as an individual: context of personal experience

When we read a text from our position as an *individual*, the context we bring to that text is affected by our life experience. Hence factors such as gender, age, ethnicity, education, family, friendships, occupation, culture, ideology and religion may all play a part in the way we make sense of a particular text. It is important, of course, not to make stereotypical assumptions about an individual's *reading position*, because such expectations can be disrupted. Indeed, as we saw in Chapter 1 (page 16) an *oppositional* reading of a text 'across the grain' can provide unexpected and fresh insights. Hence clichéd assumptions that male readers find a narrative written from a woman's point of view inaccessible (context of gender), or that an atheist would find devotional writing unintelligible (context of religion) cannot be supported. In reality, a complex text like *Paradise Lost* or *Hamlet* or *Ulysses* can be *read* in many different ways, from widely differing reader *positions.* We have selected four key factors in individual experience to look at in more detail in the *context of reading*: gender, age, ethnicity and ideology/religion.

a Gender

In the rest of this section we shall look briefly at each of the contextual factors listed above which can affect our *reading as an individual*, starting with *gender*. (By *gender* we mean the *social* meanings of *biological* difference.) How important gender is to our reading of texts will depend on how central we think it is to human social experience. If we think gender is everything, and that men and women's experience of life is entirely different, then the *reading position* of a man will always differ from the *reading position* of a female reader. It is important to note, however, that male and female readers can go against gender expectations, and learn how to *read as a man* or *read as a woman*, should this be a fruitful route to better understanding of a text.

This activity explores the gendered reading of two texts, one twentieth century, one sixteenth century. Your task is to read each carefully, bearing in mind that you are twenty-first-century readers, and then answer the following questions.

a How does Lawrence appeal to both male and female readers in this passage? Find evidence in the text of his adopting male and female perspectives on the action.

b In this passage, at the end of the play, Shakespeare shows the 'shrewish' Katherina apparently reconciled with her new husband Petruchio's 'taming'. Do you think male and female members of a modern audience would 'read' this speech in the same way? Give examples to support your view.

TEXT 1

She had only one desire now, to go to the clearing in the wood. The rest was a kind of painful dream. But sometimes she was kept all day at Wragby, by her duties as a hostess. And then she felt as if she too were going blank, just blank and insane.

... She arrived at the clearing flushed and semi-conscious. The keeper was there, in his shirt-sleeves, just closing up the coops for the night, so the little occupants were safe.

... The keeper, squatting beside her, was also watching with an amused face the bold little bird in her hand. Suddenly he saw a tear fall on her wrist.

... Her face was averted, and she was crying blindly, in all the anguish of her generation's forlornness. His heart melted suddenly, like a drop of fire, and he put out his hand and laid his fingers on her knee.

'You shouldn't cry!' he said softly.

D.H. Lawrence *Lady Chatterley's Lover* (1928)

TEXT 2

Katherina ... I am asham'd that women are so simple
To offer war where they should kneel for peace,
Or seek for rule, supremacy, and sway,
When they are bound to serve, love, and obey.
Why are our bodies soft, and weak, and smooth,
Unapt to toil and trouble in the world,
But that our soft conditions and our hearts
Should well agree with our external parts?
Come, come, you froward and unable worms,
My mind hath been as big as one of yours,
My heart as great, my reason haply more,
To bandy word for word and frown for frown.
But now I see our lances are but straws,
Our strength as weak, our weakness past compare,
That seeming to be most which we indeed least are.
Then vail your stomachs, for it is no boot,
And place your hands below your husband's foot.
In token of which duty, if he please,
My hand is ready, may it do him ease.
Petruchio Why there's a wench! Come on, and kiss me, Kate.

Shakespeare *The Taming of the Shrew* (Act V Sc.2)

b Age

Reading as a child and reading as an adult are not only different reading positions but can also produce different readings of texts. Some texts can support both perspectives, such as *Alice in Wonderland*, *The Hobbit* and even *Gulliver's Travels*. For example, in *Alice*, episodes like the Mad Hatter's Tea Party and the Trial Scene can be 'read' and enjoyed by adults as well as children. There is also no doubt that texts can be read more satisfactorily at the 'right' age, however annoying it is to be informed of this in childhood or adolescence by an adult. ("You'll enjoy that when you're older!" is an irritatingly accurate remark to recall, when it proves to be true!) Nineteenth-century novels seem to be peculiarly susceptible to this kind of difficulty. To some extent it is because children find certain aspects of adult experience dull or unimaginable. However, texts which grip adults and children alike are to be celebrated.

ACTIVITY 18

Look at the following extract from *Alice in Wonderland* and answer the following questions.

a What would a child find appealing and amusing in the passage?

b What would an adult find appealing and amusing in the passage?

c What differences and similarities are there between the two readings?

'I've been to a day-school, too,' said Alice. 'You needn't be so proud as all that.'
'With extras?' asked the Mock Turtle, a little anxiously.
'Yes,' said Alice: 'we learned French and music.'
'And washing?' said the Mock Turtle.
'Certainly not!' said Alice indignantly.
'Ah! Then yours wasn't a really good school,' said the Mock Turtle in a tone of great relief. 'Now, at *ours*, they had, at the end of the bill, "French, music, *and washing –* extra."'
'You couldn't have wanted it much,' said Alice; 'living at the bottom of the sea.'
'I couldn't afford to learn it,' said the Mock Turtle, with a sigh. 'I only took the regular course.'
'What was that?' inquired Alice.
'Reeling and Writhing, of course, to begin with,' the Mock Turtle replied; 'and then the different branches of Arithmetic – Ambition, Distraction, Uglification, and Derision.'
'I never heard of "Uglification," Alice ventured to say. 'What is it?'
The Gryphon lifted up both its paws in surprise. 'Never heard of uglifying!' it exclaimed. 'You know what to beautify is, I suppose?'
'Yes,' said Alice doubtfully: 'it means – to – make – anything – prettier.'
'Well, then,' the Gryphon went on, 'if you don't know what to uglify is, then you *are* a simpleton.'

c Ethnicity and culture

We also *read* from the position in which our ethnicity and cultural experience situates us (unless a particular text challenges us to position ourselves differently). Before England became a colonial power in the early seventeenth century, literature in English meant literature predominantly written in England. Today English is used as their chosen literary language by writers in America, Canada, Australia, New Zealand, South Africa, East and West Africa, India, the West Indies, Scotland and Ireland. There are enormous cultural differences, and there are ethnic differences too. As individuals we need to be aware of our *own* ethnic and cultural positions when we read texts by writers from different ethnic and cultural backgrounds.

ACTIVITY 19

The following texts were written by two African-American poets in the late nineteenth century (post Civil War). Your task is to answer the questions opposite, giving reasons to support your comments.

a How do you think American readers responded when they were first published?

b How do you think British readers might respond today?

TEXT 1

The Slave Auction

The sale began – young girls were there,
    Defenceless in their wretchedness,
Whose stifled sobs of deep despair
    Revealed their anguish and distress.
And mothers stood with streaming eyes,
    And saw their dearest children sold;
Unheeded rose their bitter cries,
    While tyrant bartered them for gold.
And woman, with her love and truth –
    For these in sable forms may dwell –
Gaz'd on the husband of her youth,
    With anguish none may paint or tell.
And men, whose sole crime was their hue,
    The impress of their Maker's hand,
And frail and shrinking children, too,
    Were gathered in that mournful band.
Ye who have laid your love to rest,
    And wept above their lifeless clay,
Know not the anguish of that breast,
    Whose lov'd are rudely torn away.
Ye may not know how desolate
    Are bosoms rudely forced to part
And how a dull and heavy weight
    Will press the life-drops from the heart.

Frances E.W. Harper (1825–1911)

TEXT 2

Sympathy

I know what the caged bird feels, alas!
When the sun is bright on the upland slopes;
When the wind stirs soft through the springing grass;
And the river flows like a stream of glass

When the first bird sings and the first bud opes,
And the faint perfume from its chalice steals –
I know what the caged bird feels!

I know why the caged bird beats his wing
Till its blood is red on the cruel bars;
For he must fly back to his perch and cling
When he fain would be on the bough a-swing;
And a pain still throngs in the old, old scars
And they pulse again with a keener sting –
I know why he beats his wing!

I know why the caged bird sings, ah me,
When his wing is bruised and his bosom sore,
When he beats his bars and would be free;
It is not a carol of joy or glee,
But a prayer that he sends from his heart's deep core,
But a plea, that upward to heaven he flings –
I know why the caged bird sings!

Paul Laurence Dunbar (1872–1906)

d Ideology and religion

Most of us have our individual systems of belief (*ideologies*) about the social, political and spiritual frameworks of the world we live in, which may chime with or contradict the views of the people we are close to. Our beliefs tend to influence our responses not only to other people and institutions, but also to the books we read. If we are 'set in our views', no matter how well a text is written and conveys its meaning, we reject it on the basis that we don't *agree* with its ideology. If on the other hand we are willing to put aside personal opinion, we consciously *adopt a reading position* which will enable us to make coherent sense of it.

ACTIVITY 20

The following texts all reveal (to a greater or lesser degree) the ideological position of the writer. Text 1 is by Nancy Mitford, herself a daughter of the aristocracy, who writes a comic but relatively sympathetic account of the troubles of one particular aristocratic family just before and during World War 2. Text 2 is by the late nineteenth-century poet, Jesuit priest and Catholic convert, Gerard Manley Hopkins. Text 3 is by R.S. Thomas, a poet-priest who lived in the heart of rural Wales.

Your task is to examine your own responses as readers (sympathetic or otherwise) to the political and religious ideologies explicit in these texts, by answering the questions below.

a Which text do you find most appealing? What are your reasons?
b Which text do you find least appealing? Again, give your reasons.
c Which text succeeds best in conveying its message? Give reasons to support your view.

TEXT 1

I am obliged to begin this story with a brief account of the Hampton family, because it is necessary to emphasize the fact once and for all that the Hamptons were very grand as well as very rich. A glance at Burke or at Debrett would be quite enough to make this clear, but these large volumes are not always available, while the books on the subject by Lord Montdore's brother-in-law, Boy Dougdale, are all out of print. His great talent for snobbishness and small talent for literature have produced three detailed studies of his wife's forebears, but they can only be read now by asking a bookseller to get them at second hand ... *Georgiana Lady Montdore and her Circle, The Magnificent Montdores* and *Old Chronicles of Hampton,* I have beside me as I write. ... It must be said that when this terrible trilogy first came out it had quite a vogue with the lending library public.

Glossary: 'Burke' and 'Debrett' both refer to histories of the British aristocracy, published annually.

Nancy Mitford *Love in a Cold Climate* (1949)

TEXT 2

God's Grandeur

The world is charged with the grandeur of God.
   It will flame out, like shining from shook foil;
   It gathers to a greatness, like the ooze of oil
Crushed. Why do men now not reck his rod?
Generations have trod, have trod, have trod;
   And all is seared with trade; bleared, smeared with toil;
   And wears man's smudge and shares man's smell: the soil
Is bare now, nor can foot feel, being shod.
And for all this, nature is never spent;
   There lives the dearest freshness deep down things
And though the last lights off the black West went
   Oh, morning, at the brown brink eastward, springs –
Because the Holy Ghost over the bent
   world broods with warm breast and with ah! bright wings.

Gerard Manley Hopkins (1844–1889)

TEXT 3

The Belfry

I have seen it standing up grey,
Gaunt, as though no sunlight
Could ever thaw out the music
Of its great bell; terrible
In its own way, for religion
Is like that. There are times
When a black frost is upon
One's whole being, and the heart
In its bone belfry hangs and is dumb.

But who is to know? Always,
Even in winter in the cold
Of a stone church, on his knees
Someone is praying, whose prayers fall
Steadily through the hard spell
Of weather that is between God
And himself. Perhaps they are warm rain
That brings the sun and afterwards flowers
On the raw graves and throbbing of bells.

R.S. Thomas (1913–2000)

Reading as a member of society: context of public experience

We have looked at various factors likely to affect an individual reader's perspective on a text, leaving to one side the effects family and friends, education and occupation may have on us as readers. We shall take account of these in this section, under the umbrella of a reader's *social experience*. Our social attitudes tend to be mediated through social groups, both small (the family) and large (the community). Consciously or not, we may well be influenced by these social attitudes in our reading of a text. For example, the Cold War made spy-thrillers a particularly popular genre in the 1970s (e.g. *The Spy Who Came in from the Cold* by John Le Carré, and Ian Fleming's Bond books). Fifty years earlier, adventure stories like John Buchan's *The Thirty Nine Steps* (1915) reflected a heroic ex-colonial world, now unrecognisable. Other examples of public attitudes influencing the *reading position* of their audience are the violent reaction to sexual frankness in James Joyce's *Ulysses* (1922) and D.H. Lawrence's *Lady Chatterley's Lover* (1928). Both writers were regarded as scandalous and the books banned: indeed, *Ulysses* was not published in Britain until 1936, and *Lady Chatterley's Lover* had to wait until 1958 for an unexpurgated British edition.

We can see that social attitudes can strongly affect the reading position of the public. Today, increasingly graphic representation of human sexuality in literary texts reflects the increasingly liberal positioning of the readers. It is also interesting to note how a relatively recent social attitude like *political correctness* affects the way a text situates a reader. We can feel reluctant to reveal negative attitudes towards a book if this implies racist, anti-feminist, or any other kind of prejudice against a disadvantaged minority within society. James Finn Garner, author of *Politically Correct Bedtime Stories* (1994) takes wicked advantage of this in his highly successful re-writing of traditional tales like Cinderella or The Three Bears.

ACTIVITY 21

The following extracts are both taken from the opening pages of their respective texts. They describe two very different social environments: Ireland in the early 1930s, and East London in the late 1980s. Your task is:

a to decide the reading position which suits you best (from the *context of individual experience* or from the *context of social experience*) for each extract

b to provide textual detail to support your chosen reading position for each extract

c to compare notes with other members of your group.

TEXT 1

Not even snowfall could make Leyton look lovely. Sootfall was what it was; a fine drizzle of ash that sprinkled the pavements and terrace rooftops, dusting the rusty railings and faded awnings of the few remaining shops along the high road. ... Grey flecks nested in the grooves of the shutters of the boarded up homes, abandoned when new homes were put down and old ladies died; they settled silently on the graves in the choked churchyard, giving grace and shadow to long-unread inscriptions – Edna, Beloved Wife; Edward, Sleeps with the Angels – and dressed the withered cedars in almost-mourning robes of almost-black. Pigeons shook their heads, sneezing, blinking away the icy specks, claws skittering on the unfamiliar roof which had once been the reassuring flat red tiles of the Methodist church and was now a gleaming minaret, topped by a metal sickle moon. The moon at midday, dark snow and nowhere to perch. No wonder they said Coo.

An old man picked up a frozen milk bottle from his front step and held it up to the light, squinting at the petrified pearly sea beyond the glass. He'd seen an ocean like that once, in the navy or on the TV, he couldn't remember which now.

. . . And then he heard them. Nothing more than an echo at first, muted by wind and traffic, but he felt the sound, like you always do when it brings the past with it. Clop-clop, there it was, no mistaking it.

The horse turned the corner into his road, white enough to shame what fell from the sky, carrying what looked like a Christmas tree on its back. There was a man in the middle of the tinsel, pearls hanging down over his brown skin, suspended from a cartoon-size turban. He held a nervous small boy, similarly attired, on his lap. Behind him, a group of men of assorted heights and stomach sizes, grins as stiff as their new suits, attempted a half-dance half-jog behind the swishing tail, their polished shoes slipping in the slush. A fat man in a pink jacket held a drum around his neck and banged it with huge palms, like a punishment, daring anyone not to join in . . .

. . . Swamped, thought the old man; someone said that once, we'll be swamped by them. But it isn't like that, wet and soggy like Hackney Marshes. It's silent and gentle, so gradual you hardly notice it at all until you look up and see that everything's different.

Meera Syal Life isn't all ha ha hee hee (1999)

TEXT 2

My father and mother should have stayed in New York where they met and married and where I was born. Instead they returned to Ireland when I was four, my brother Malachy, three, the twins, Oliver and Eugene, barely one, and my sister, Margaret, dead and gone.

When I look back at my childhood I wonder how I survived at all. It was, of course, a miserable childhood: the happy childhood is hardly worth your while. Worse than the ordinary miserable childhood is the miserable Irish childhood, and worse yet is the miserable Irish Catholic childhood.

People everywhere brag and whimper about the woes of their early years, but nothing can compare with the Irish version: the poverty; the shiftless loquacious alcoholic father; the pious defeated mother moaning by the fire; pompous priests; bullying schoolmasters; the English and the terrible things they did to us for eight hundred long years.

Above all – we were wet.

Out in the Atlantic Ocean great sheets of rain gathered to drift slowly up the River Shannon and settle forever in Limerick. The rain dampened the city from the Feast of the Circumcision to New Year's Eve. It created a cacophony of hacking coughs, bronchial rattles, asthmatic wheezes, consumptive croaks. It turned noses into fountains, lungs into bacterial sponges.

. . . From October to April the walls of Limerick glistened with the damp. Clothes never dried: tweed and woolen clothes housed living things, sometimes sprouted mysterious vegetations.

. . . The rain drove us into the church – our refuge, our strength, our only dry place. At Mass, benediction, novenas, we huddled in great damp clumps, dozing through priest drone, while steam rose again from our clothes to mingle with the sweetness of incense, flowers and candles.

Limerick gained a reputation for piety, but we knew it was only the rain.

Frank McCourt *Angela's Ashes* (1997)

Summary

As our study of *context* deepens, in this chapter we have investigated what 'makes us tick' as readers – what we read, why we choose certain kinds of books and how we expect to benefit from our reading. The *context of reading* enables us to make sense of the texts we read, not only as individuals with unique idiosyncrasies and preferences, but also as vital members of society. This is not to say that as readers, our position may not be against the grain, or with a particular perspective deriving from specific circumstances – i.e. as an examination candidate, or an academic who is a professional student of literature, There is always room for new ways of *reading texts* – almost as many as there are people reading them! What we can be fairly sure is that there are far fewer people *writing* literary texts than there are people reading them. In the next chapter we shall be looking at the *context of writing.*

Text references page 23–26
1. J.K. Rowling *Harry Potter and the Philosopher's Stone*
2. Bill Bryson *Down Under*
3. J.B. Priestley *An Inspector Calls*
4. Charles Dickens *The Pickwick Papers*
5. P.D. James *Death of an Expert Witness*
6. Zadie Smith *White Teeth*
7. Alfred Lord Tennyson *In Memoriam*
8. John Betjeman *Slough* from *Collected Poems*

3 Context from the Writer's Position

In Chapters 1 and 2 we established some working definitions of *context* and *text*, and explored the complexities of reading position in relation to texts. By first focusing on reading position in Chapter 2, we started at the 'far end' of the communicative process *author–text–reader*, for reasons we explained at the time. Now in this chapter we shall return to 'normal order' and focus on *writing position* in relation to a text. The chapter is divided into three parts. The first section explores the role of the author/writer, in some depth, and particularly the difference between texts which are *lisible* ('readerly' or closed – the audience does nothing but remain distant and *read*) and texts which are *scriptible* ('writerly' – or open – the audience may be required to be involved creatively themselves). The second section investigates *context* from the *writer's* position; in the third and final section a set of strategies or 'model' is proposed, which is applicable to any text (spoken or written, literary or non-literary) in order to determine its *context(s)*.

Part 1: Authors and Texts: Roles and Definitions

a The role of the author/writer

What does the term 'author' mean?

Although we usually associate the term 'author' with writing, and particularly the writing of literature, in fact the word can have a more generalised meaning, referring to someone who brings something into being, who produces an action or state of things. This reflects the word's etymology; it derives from the Latin verb *augere* (meaning 'to increase, to produce'), and the Latin noun *auctor* (meaning someone who produces or creates something, 'makes things happen'). This wider non-literary meaning appears in current expressions like 'well, he's the *author* of his own troubles' as well as in earlier usage, as the Anglican *Book of Common Prayer* (1662), where God is described as 'the *author* and giver of all good things'. Plainly nothing to do with creative writing!

How do we recognise an 'author'?

Nevertheless, our prime concern is with the *author as writer or producer of a text*, and in particular a *literary text* – in other words, a 'special sort of writing'. To be recognised as an *author*, a writer has to work within the shared knowledge and conventions of the language community in which he or she functions, and in which a text can be circulated, read and understood. For example, in some societies one literary genre (e.g. the 'football novel' like Nick Hornby's *Fever Pitch*) might be entirely unknown, because it did not 'fit' the cultural expectations and experience of that social group (e.g. American baseball enthusiasts), whereas in other cultural communities this genre might be the most popular mode of literary expression!

Authorship past and present – the issue of anonymity

Incidentally, it seems that the rise of the concept of the *author* is relatively modern. In the Middle Ages, anonymous authorship was commonplace and generally accepted – it's not just because early records are inadequate that many pre-Renaissance texts are ascribed to *Anon*. However, with the gradual rise of individualism (starting in the Renaissance, developing through the Age of Reason, and culminating in the Romantic period), the idea of individual, named authorship has also grown stronger and stronger. Even so, there are still special cases where anonymity is chosen by individual authors. In the eighteenth and nineteenth centuries just being female was a sufficient reason for hiding one's identity under various guises, including: simple gender description ('A Lady'); gender/social class description ('A Lady of Quality'); gender/patriotic description ('A.L.O.E. A Lady of England'); a different female name from the author's ('Clemence Dane', 'Gertrude', 'Hesba Stretton'); a male name ('Currer, Ellis and Acton Bell' for Charlotte, Emily and Anne Brontë, and 'George Eliot' for Marian Evans). The reasons for this desire for anonymity and/or use of pseudonyms are predominantly social rather than literary. Until relatively recently (apart from during the two World Wars) the general public saw women's place to be in the home. Their role was in the private, not the public domain, and any inappropriate publicity (i.e. being the author of a book) might expose a woman to charges of impropriety and scandal.

What are the public rights and responsibilities of 'the author'?

There are other problems, too, apart from the ones discussed above. Is the author simply a person who wrote a text, or does the general public have special expectations of 'authors'? In the last decade Salman Rushdie, a well-known novelist writing in English, had a very public problem. He became the object of a *fatwa* (death penalty imposed by a Muslim judicial authority) because he wrote an allegedly blasphemous book, *The Satanic Verses* (1988). The *fatwa* (only recently withdrawn) resulted in Rushdie seeking police protection and leading a hunted, underground existence for over ten years. Of course, Rushdie's predicament received the full glare of media publicity, adding to his difficulties. But it all happened because he is a well-known author whose personal and individual life became virtual public property, and of whom the general public apparently had certain fixed (and unfulfilled) expectations.

Is the author alive or dead?

Indeed, some distinguished theorists have challenged the power of the author, including the French critic Roland Barthes who in 1977 published an article entitled 'The Death of the Author'. Seeing the intimate link between author and text as a rather dangerous and narrowing kind of *individualism*, Barthes claimed that it is the *language of a text* which speaks to the reader, not the individual author. The responsibility and power of the reader is such, Barthes continues, that 'the birth of the reader must be at the cost of the death of the author'. How far one can go along with this extreme view is a matter of individual choice.

The implied author

But this is not the time for us all to give up on the 'author' and go home! Most readers feel that the author is important, and develop their own sense of the implied author. Hawthorn (page 12) defines this feeling as 'that sense of the creating author behind a literary work that the reader builds up on the basis of the individual work.' Perhaps the classical example of the implied author is Shakespeare – we tend to make guesses about the sort of man he might have been, based on the extraordinarily richness and variety of his output as dramatist and poet. Added to these kinds of intuitions about Shakespeare, of course, are innumerable biographies, reflecting the detective work done by literary historians anxious to flesh out the bare bones of factual evidence.

ACTIVITY 22

The texts below have *no named author*. They were all published anonymously or under a pseudonym (approximate dates have been provided). Your task is to read them carefully, and then with a partner try to work out the *implied author*.

Look for clues under the following headings:

- authorial voice and his/her relationship with text/author of text
- attitude to topic/ subject matter
- organisation of text
- language choice including figurative language.

TEXT 1 (early seventeenth century)

Epitaph: on Sir Walter Raleigh at his Execution

Great heart, who taught thee so to dye?
Death yielding thee the victory?
Where took'st thee leave of life? if there,
How could'st thou be so freed from feare?
But sure thou dy'st and quit'st the state
Of flesh and blood before thy fate.
Else what a miracle were wrought,
To triumph both in flesh and thought?
I saw in every stander by,
Pale death, life onely in thine eye:
Th'example that thou left'st was then,
We look for when thou dy'est agen.
   Farewell, truth shall thy story say,
We dy'd, thou only liv'dst that day.

COMMENTARY

Walter Raleigh was executed in 1618, so the poem was probably written after this date by a friend or sympathiser (*authorial voice*: 'Great Heart'). He had already been imprisoned in the Tower of London from 1603–1616 on trumped up charges (together with his wife and family). A brief and disastrous expedition to South America and back led to re-imprisonment and death. His demeanour at his death makes it seem that he had faced and won a victory over death already, that he was the only 'live' person there, the bystanders were 'dead' with grief (*attitude to subject*). The *implied author* is someone of wit and education (use of antithesis) who knew of Raleigh's previous sufferings and hints that justice was not done, that the truth will out (as indeed it did). We have a strong sense of the writer's personal sense of grief and loss, and of his great admiration of Raleigh.

The text is structured to reach a climactic point in the final paradoxical line 'We dy'd, thou only liv'dst that day'.

TEXT 2 (eighteenth century)

To a Proud Beauty

Imperious fool! Think not because you're fair,
That you so much above my converse are,
What though the gallants sing your praises loud,
And with false plaudits make you vainly proud?
Though they may tell you all adore your eyes,
And every heart's your willing sacrifice;

Or spin the flatt'ry finer, and persuade
Your easy vanity, that we were made
For foils to make your lustre shine more bright,
And must pay homage to your dazzling light,
Yet know whatever stories they may tell,
All you can boast, is, to be pretty well; ...

TEXT 3 (late seventeeth century)

Gunpowder Plot Day

Please to remember
The Fifth of November,
Gunpowder treason and plot;
I see no reason
Why gunpowder treason
Should ever be forgot.

TEXT 4 (nineteenth century)

'Come hither, child,' said the old Earl of Courtland to his daughter, as, in obedience to his summons, she entered his study: 'come hither, I say; I wish to have some serious conversation with you: so dismiss your dogs, shut the door, and sit down here.'

Lady Juliana called for the footman to take Venus; bade Pluto be quiet, like a darling, under the sofa; and, taking Cupid in her arms, assured his lordship he need fear no disturbance from the sweet creatures, and that she would be all attention to his commands – kissing her cherished pug as she spoke.

'You are now, I think, seventeen, Juliana,' said his lordship, in a solemn important tone.

'And a half, papa.'

'It is therefore time you should be thinking of establishing yourself in the world. Have you ever turned your thoughts that way?'

'N – no, papa, not exactly in the way of establishing myself,' replied the lady, hesitatingly.

'That is well; you have left that for me to do, like a good, wise little girl, as you are. Is it not so, my pretty Jule?'

TEXT 5 (mid-nineteenth century)

A dialogue I'll tell thee as true as my life,
Between a coal-owner and a poor pitman's wife.
As she was a'travelling all on the highway,
She met a coal-owner and this did she say,
Derry down, down, down derry down.

'Good morning, Lord Firedamp,' this woman she said,
I'll do you no harm, sir, so don't be afraid,
If you've been where I've been the most of my life,
You wouldn't turn pale at the poor pitman's wife.'
Derry down, down, down derry down.

'Then where do you come from?' the owner he cries.
'I come from hell,' the poor woman replies.
'If you come from hell, then come tell me right plain,
How you contrived to get out again.'
Derry down, down, down derry down.

'Aye, the way I got out, the truth will I tell.
They're turning the poor folk all out of hell.
This is to make room for the rich wicked race,
For there is a great number of them in that place.
   Derry down, down, down derry down.

'And the coal-owners is the next on command
To arrive in hell, as I understand,
For I heard the old devil say as I came out,
The coal-owners all had received their rout.'
   Derry down, down, down derry down . . . .

b 'Writerly' and 'readerly' texts

We've already given a brief account of the difference between *lisible* (readerly) and *scriptible* (writerly) texts (page 38), and we shall explore this difference in a little more detail, because understanding it can extend our understanding of *context*. In *readerly* texts the reader and the author *share* expectations, *recognise* the conventions of the chosen genre, and *rely* on them being there. Barthes thinks that the effect of this shared understanding has its limitations, and can close down or fix the range of possible meanings. For example, if you read a Mills and Boon romance you and the author share certain expectations, and the introduction of science fiction or thriller genre characteristics would not please reader or author. In *writerly* texts, on the other hand, literary conventions are violated, expectations flouted, and the reader is made to work hard to understand the text, almost as though he or she were *writing* it again for themselves.

It's not surprising that the majority of literary texts up to the twentieth century could be described as *readerly*. However transforming and innovative their individual genius, writers like Shakespeare, Aphra Behn, Fielding, Charlotte Brontë, Donne and Tennyson work *within the conventions and expectations of their chosen genre*. It's not until the rise of the *modernism* movement in the 1920s that writers consistently chose to challenge tradition, and produce *writerly* texts like *Ulysses* or *Mrs Dalloway*.

Nor was this challenge limited to literature – Picasso and Schoenberg in their respective modes of painting and music broke the mould just as much as writers like Virginia Woolf and James Joyce. The latter experimented with the 'stream of consciousness' narrative technique, where a character's thoughts and feelings are linked together by random association (as we do ourselves, mentally hopping between a recent text message, the next English homework, weekend plans and an argument at home). The reader does have to 'work' a little to fathom the meanings – at least at first! Modernist writers of fiction came up with other ways of challenging their readers, including multiple-voice narrative (lots of different viewpoints on the events), non-chronological narrative structure (using flashback and flash forward), and 'alternative' endings. Similarly, poets and dramatists experimented with new ways of communicating meaning and challenging genre conventions.

ACTIVITY 23

Listed below are extracts from a range of literary genres. The purpose of the exercise is to decide (with a partner) which is more like a *readerly* text and which is more like a *writerly* text. In order to help you to decide, you may like to use the following questions as guidelines:

a Identify the genre of the extract/text (i.e. fiction, poetry, drama – more specific genre detail if possible)

b Does the writer broadly match your expectations of the genre in the extract/text? Give examples to support your view.

c Does the writer surprise or challenge your genre expectations in any way? Give examples to support your view.

d You should now be able to decide if the extract/passage is *readerly* or *writerly*!

TEXT 1

She felt very young; and at the same time unspeakably aged. She sliced like a knife through everything; at the same time was at the outside looking on. She had a perpetual sense, as she watched the taxicabs, of being far out, out, far out to sea and alone; she always had the feeling that it was very, very dangerous to live even one day. Not that she thought herself clever, or much out of the ordinary. How she had got through life on the few twigs of knowledge Fraulein Daniels gave them she could not think. She knew nothing; no language, no history; she scarcely read a book now, except memoirs in bed; and yet to her it was absolutely absorbing; all this; the cabs passing; and she would not say of Peter, she would not say of herself, I am this, I am that.

TEXT 2

Sonnet to Sleep

O soft embalmer of the still midnight,
　　Shutting with careful fingers and benign
Our gloom-pleas'd eyes embower'd from the light,
　　Enshaded in forgetfulness divine:
O soothest Sleep! if so it please thee, close,
　　In midst of this thine hymn, my willing eyes,
Or wait the Amen ere thy poppy throws
　　Around my bed its lulling charities.
Then save me or the passed day will shine
　　Upon my pillow, breeding many woes:
Save me from curious conscience, that still hoards
　　Its strength for darkness, burrowing like the mole;
Turn the key deftly in the oiled wards,
　　And seal the hushed casket of my soul.

TEXT 3

Lydgate's conceit was of the arrogant sort, never simpering, never impertinent, but massive in its claims and benevolently contemptuous. He would do a great deal for noodles, being sorry for them, and feeling quite sure they could have no power over him ... Lydgate's spots of commonness lay in the complexion of his prejudices, which in spite of noble intentions and sympathy, were half of them such as are found in ordinary men of the world: that distinction of mind which belonged to his intellectual ardour, did not penetrate his feeling and judgment about furniture, or women, or the desirability of its being known (without his telling) that he was better born than other country surgeons. He did not mean to think of furniture at present; but whenever he did so, it was to be feared that neither biology nor schemes of reform would lift him above the vulgarity of feeling that there would be an incompatibility in his furniture not being of the best.

TEXT 4

... For I have known them all already, known them all –
Have known the evenings, mornings, afternoons,
I have measured out my life with coffee spoons;
I know the voices dying with a dying fall
Beneath the music of a farther room.
   So how should I presume?

And I have known the eyes already, known them all –
The eyes that fix you in a formulated phrase,
And when I am formulated, sprawling on a pin,
When I am pinned and wriggling on the wall,
Then how should I begin
To spit out all the butt-ends of my days and ways?
   And how should I presume?

... I should have been a pair of ragged claws
Scuttling across the floors of silent seas.

TEXT 5

Through the fence, between the curling flower spaces, I could see them hitting. They were coming toward where the flag was and I went along the fence. Luster was hunting in the grass by the flower tree. They took the flag out, and they were hitting. Then they put the flag back and they went to the table, and he hit and the other hit. Then they went on, and I went along the fence. Luster came away from the flower tree and we went along the fence and they stopped and we stopped and I looked through the fence while Luster was hunting in the grass.

   'Here, caddie.' He hit. They went away across the pasture. I held to the fence and watched them going away.

   'Listen at you, now.' Luster said. 'Ain't you something, thirty-three years old, going on that way. After I done went all the way to town to buy you that cake. Hush up that moaning. Ain't you going to help me find that quarter so I can go to the show tonight.'

Part 2: Context from the Writer's Position

In Chapter 2 when we were exploring context from the reader's position, we adopted a dual approach, firstly considering context from the reader's position as an individual, and secondly viewing context from the individual's perspective as a member of society. We shall structure our discussion of the writer's position in the same way.

a The writer's position as an individual

Why do people become writers? If you go to your local public library any September, you will almost certainly find listed under local leisure activities and/or adult education, classes in *creative writing*, offering potential writers opportunities to experiment with a wide range of genres, from poetry and fiction to plays, film scripts, even biography and autobiography. Every year creative writing classes are offered, and every year they are well-subscribed. Apparently there are a lot of people nation-wide who are keen to develop their writing skills; and if you go up a notch, you will find writers' workshops (often residential) are equally popular, especially if they're taught by practicing and published writers. At university level there are creative writing degrees, and at post-graduate level such famous courses as the MA in Creative Writing at the University of East Anglia. Furthermore, there is a huge and crucial reference book, sufficiently popular to be published annually (at over 700 pages) which succeeds in fulfilling the needs of its large target audience. *The Writer's Handbook* (2000) provides current advice and information on topics ranging from poetry magazines and literary agents to publishers, literary rights and how to avoid being libellous. The steady demand for a book like this reflects the commitment of numerous *authors as individuals*.

Where does the desire to write come from? Are we all potential writers, or is it a special quality which people recognise in themselves, and which drives them forwards? The Irish writer Edna O'Brien describes her position below (quoted in *A Portrait of the Artist as a Young Girl* (1986) ed. John Quinn, Methuen):

I think one is born a writer. I know that circumstances alter the subject of one's fiction, but the writing is there from the beginning, all the same. It is somehow that living is incomplete until it is fastened through words into a piece of fiction or drama. I always knew that I would be a writer – for as long as I can remember I knew that I would write. I didn't know what it meant to be a writer but I knew that my reality, my life and my fate would be lived out through words: 'In the beginning was the Word ...'

This kind of view is not unfamiliar – many other writers, past and present, have described a sense of destiny from an early age. Others describe a lonely childhood, with books providing company and imaginative stimulus – the Brontë children are a classic example of this. Their elaborate stories about the imaginary worlds of Angria and Gondal provided early opportunities for exploring character, plot and description, later demonstrated in novels like *Jane Eyre, The Tenant of Wildfell Hall* and *Wuthering Heights.*

Our next question is *why* do people choose to write? If you have ever written yourself (voluntarily, not at the request of a teacher) you may have found it enjoyable to invent characters and create a world in which they live and where exciting things happen. Your imagination may have been stimulated by books and magazines, by films, cartoons or television – or your ideas might be entirely of your own invention. Children's writing often reproduces in more romantic or dramatic form the world they themselves inhabit; adult writers, on the other hand, whilst using similar strategies, have many different purposes; they may have a story to tell, issues to raise, ideologies, cultures and attitudes to challenge, something to explain or describe. Above all, they have an urgent need to communicate – even if it seems to be only to themselves.

ACTIVITY 24

Below is a range of quotations from some twentieth-century writers of fiction about the process of writing. Read them through carefully.

Do these explanations match any novels you are familiar with? Discuss in groups.

It seems to me that my books are ideas-driven – they are a dramatic expression of what interests me or preoccupies me or obsesses me at the time. (Hilary Mantel)

If I were asked what is the essence of story-telling, I would say it is a simple thing: the relating of something strange. (Graham Swift)

Creating people is a fascinating business. Some characters start to live and breathe almost without one's help, whereas others – despite huffings and puffings on the author's part – stubbornly refuse to spring to life and remain stillbirths. (Deborah Moggach)

Of course you want to hear their voices. Having summoned up these human beings, you want to know what they sound like. (Penelope Fitzgerald)

For most of my adult life I resisted writing.
I fought an 'internal battle' with the words, characters and lives that inhabited my mind, and at times threatened to devour it. I superimposed on this assault of the imagination, initially – and most strangely – a business career in magazine publishing, then a career as a theatre producer – accompanied by a short sortie into television … In the summer of 1989 I finally collapsed on to the page. As though insane with relief, the words poured from their prison. … The cause of my long terror of writing lies deeper than I care to go … Perhaps I knew my writing came from the 'edge of things', and I recognised it to be dangerous. (Josephine Hart)

Why bother to write fiction? There are so many answers and every writer will give you a different one. To earn a crust? To satisfy our basic instinct, since we lived in caves and hunted mammoths, to tell stories and enjoy the fact that people gather round to listen? To make some sort of order out of a chaotic universe, or to expel some old devils from inside us and send them out into the world? Whatever our motives one thing is certain: our work can't be any good unless we tell the truth about life as we see it. (John Mortimer)

All quotations from C. Boylan ed. *The Agony and the Ego* (1993)

Telling the truth, attempting to make order out of chaos, writing 'on the edge', relating something strange – these are all accounts of the act of communication from the point of view of the *author as individual*. Clearly the individual experience of the writers above reflects the context of their personal lives just as the context of *our* individual lives affected us as *readers*. The poems below reveal the individual *physical vulnerability* of Milton and of Keats, but enable readers to respond in more general terms. Milton describes the onset of blindness in early middle age, Keats his fears of premature death ending his creative ambitions (his younger brother and mother had both died of consumption).

ACTIVITY 25

Read the following sonnets through carefully, and then (working with a partner), answer these questions:

a Both poets have experienced pain and uncertainty, and explore their feelings about this in the sonnets. What conclusion does each poet arrive at about their situation?

b Compare the figurative language and other literary techniques used by each poet to convey his thoughts and feelings. Refer to specific examples in both poems.

c Can you find any references to other texts (*intertextuality*) in either sonnet? If so, what might be the purpose of the allusion/reference within the poem?

TEXT 1

When I consider how my light is spent,
　Ere half my days, in this dark world and wide,
　And that one talent which is death to hide,
　Lodged with me useless, though my soul more bent

To serve therewith my Maker, and present
　My true account, lest he returning chide;
　'Doth God exact day-labour, light denied?'
　I fondly ask; but Patience to prevent

That murmur, soon replies, 'God doth not need
　Either man's work or his own gifts; who best
　Bear his mild yoke, they serve him best. His state

Is kingly. Thousands at this bidding speed
　And post o'er land and ocean without rest:
　They also serve who only stand and wait.'

TEXT 2

When I have fears that I may cease to be
　Before my pen has glean'd my teeming brain,
Before high piled books, in charact'ry,
　Hold like rich garners the full ripen'd grain;
When I behold, upon the night's starr'd face,
　Huge cloudy symbols of a high romance,
And think that I may never live to trace
　Their shadows, with the magic hand of chance;

When I feel, fair creature of an hour,
    That I shall never look upon thee more,
Never have relish in the fairy power
    Of unreflecting love; – then on the shore
Of the wide world I stand alone, and think
    Till love and fame to nothingness do sink.

There are numerous other examples of the author using individual experience in his or her writing: for example, Anne Brontë's portrait of the heroine's drunken and abusive husband (*The Tenant of Wildfell Hall* [1848]) is partly based on her own brother, Branwell; similarly, in the twentieth century we have Douglas Dunn's remarkable series of poems, *Elegies*, about his wife's illness and death.

Although it may not always be overt, personal experience is clearly an important context for a writer. Other aspects of context (gender, age, education, family experience, reading and value systems), previously explored in relation to the individual reader (page 28), are of equal importance in relation to the individual author. In the next three chapters we shall be looking at individual instances of these. There are, however, two less obvious aspects of the *context of the author as individual* which deserve our attention: the writer's choice of genre; and the position of the writer in relation to the work of other writers.

The first is not really much of a problem; although a writer's choice of genre *may* be influenced by current literary fashion (and hence be the result of social rather than personal experience), most writers choose the genre which works best in communicating what each – as an individual – has to say. The second is more serious: the writer as individual tends to feel himself or herself in the shadow of the great poets, novelists and playwrights of the past. Can a modern writer ever be 'original' in the light of past literary tradition? The American critic, Harold Bloom, sums up this fear neatly as the 'anxiety of influence'. Bloom sees this as an individual struggle for each writer. The 'strong poet' (or novelist or playwright) is the one who can *absorb* and *transform* the achievement of the past and make the new text powerful in a new way. A classic example of this is the novel *Ulysses* (1922), by James Joyce. Joyce 'rewrites' the story of the Greek hero Odysseus and his adventures after the Trojan War and sets it in early twentieth-century Dublin. The wanderings of Joyce's hero, Leopold Bloom, are narrated hour-by-hour, and his experiences 'match' some of the Greek hero's exploits (e.g. the Sirens, Circe's island). Through Joyce's *absorbing* and *transforming* skills, the Greek epic poem, the *Odyssey* is 'reborn' as a powerful new text.

ACTIVITY 26

The following activity aims **a** to give you the opportunity to sharpen up your understanding of literary genre, **b** to enable you to recognise from first-hand experience how the writer as individual 'mines' his or her own personal experience, and **c** to give you an opportunity to 'transform' a text and make it new.

a Choose two literary texts you know well. Imagine that you have to *change the genre* of each of your chosen texts. What *new* genre would you choose and what changes would you make? (possibilities: change in structure, narrative voice, setting, characterisation) Make notes on your plans and discuss them with the group.

b Choose one of the following genres (play, short story, poem/group of poems) and using some aspect of your personal experience, write on the theme of *misunderstanding*. There is no need to be *directly* autobiographical, unless that is part of your deliberate plan. The length of your writing will depend on the time you have available. (You may also wish to include a brief commentary on the ways you used personal experience and how well it worked.)

c Choose a nursery rhyme and 'make it new' by transforming it into a different genre (not necessarily literary). Read the rewritten version to the group and exchange views!

NB *Activities 26a and 26c could both be useful in preparing for coursework; 26b could actually be a coursework submission.*

b The writer's position as part of society

The context of a text from the writer's position includes not only his or her individual or personal experience, but also his or her experience as part of *society*. We shall now look at the implications of this, bearing in mind that the writer is likely to be part of the same society as the reader, and thus their experience is *shared*. The author, however, is the person who sets the act of communication going by writing the text (author–text–reader), and he or she will be influenced by their *social experience*. Sometimes a writer subscribes completely to current social attitudes and values; other writers may be highly critical of contemporary society and its culture and values, and write 'against the grain'. Writers' attitudes can range from complete acceptance to total hostility, and can be expressed in many ways, from mild irony to biting satire. Thus it is essential for us not only to be aware of the sociopolitical context of a given literary text, but also of the writer's *attitude* to his or her society.

Chaucer and Shakespeare provide two good examples of this. Written in the late fourteenth century, Chaucer's *General Prologue* to *The Canterbury Tales* (1387–8) presents a sharp critique of the Church through its more worldly representatives, the Prioress, the Monk, the Summoner, the Friar and the Pardoner, whilst evidently admiring the Christian virtues of the Knight, the Ploughman and the poor Parson. Chaucer seems to have no direct dispute with the Church, or with its theology, but beneath his narrator's ironic description of the Pardoner, we discern his angry disgust at its corrupt practices, such as the selling of pardons and penances to the poor for substantial profit. Two hundred years later, in the late sixteenth century, Shakespeare's history plays, with their focus on the early days of the Tudor dynasty, not only examine issues of kingship and the relationship between crown and state, but also address the question of succession, past and present. With Queen Elizabeth I childless, this was a burning issue for Elizabethans, especially in the 1590s, when *Henry VI Parts 1, 2 and 3*, *Richard III*, *King John*, *Richard II*, *Henry IV Parts 1 and 2* and *Henry V* were all written and produced. (Queen Elizabeth died in 1603, and King James I of England and VI of Scotland, her nephew, succeeded to the English throne.) Both Chaucer and Shakespeare can be seen to be writing *within their contemporary social context*, whilst retaining the freedom to question (overtly or covertly) aspects of this society.

ACTIVITY 27

The authors of the following extracts were very much aware of what was going on in society at the time they were writing. Each extract has a brief introduction explaining the *social context*. Read the introduction and the extracts carefully, and then answer the following questions:

a What aspect(s) of his or her society is the writer referring to in the text?
b What attitude(s) does the writer convey to us in the text?

TEXT 1
Jonathan Swift (1667–1745), famously author of *Gulliver's Travels* (1726), was an Anglo-Irish writer, priest and Dean of St Patrick's Church in Dublin. He was well known for his strongly held political views. At the time he wrote *A Modest Proposal* (1729) the Irish peasantry were starving, illiterate, harshly oppressed by the English absentee landlords and by Parliament. The full title of the text is *A Modest Proposal (for preventing the children of poor parents from being a burden to their parents or country, and for making them beneficial to the public)*.

It is a melancholy object to those who walk through this great town or travel in the country, when they see the streets, the roads, and cabin doors, crowded with beggars of the female sex, followed by three, four, or six children, all in rags and importuning every passenger for an alms. . . . I think it is agreed by all parties that this prodigious number of children in the arms, or on the backs, or at the heels of their mothers, and frequently of their fathers, is in the present deplorable state of the kingdom a very great additional grievance. . . . I shall now therefore humbly propose my own thoughts, which I hope will not be liable to the least objection. I have been assured by a very knowing American of my acquaintance in London, that young healthy child well nursed is at a year old a most delicious, nourishing and wholesome food, whether stewed, roasted, baked or boiled; and I make no doubt that it will equally serve in a fricassee or a ragout.

TEXT 2
Siegfried Sassoon (1886–1967) came from a privileged background, and fought as an officer in the trenches in World War 1. He became progressively more hostile to the war, especially after the horror of the 1916 Somme offensive, in which his outstanding bravery led to the award of the Military Cross. After periods in hospital (including Craiglockhart psychiatric hospital, where he met and encouraged the poet Wilfred Owen), Sassoon made a public declaration of his criticism of the war effort, throwing the MC into the Mersey. He returned to the front, and was invalided out in spring 1918.

The General

'Good-morning; good-morning!' the General said
When we met him last week on our way to the line.
Now the soldiers he smiled at are most of 'em dead,
And we're cursing his staff for incompetent swine.
'He's a cheery old card,' grunted Harry to Jack
As they slogged up to Arras with rifle and pack.

*

But he did for them both by his plan of attack.

TEXT 3
Grace Nichols (1950 –) was born and educated in Guyana, but came to Britain in 1977 to work as a journalist. She has published several collections of poems focusing on the experience of the West Indian in exile (*The Fat Black Woman's Poems*) and on the slave-history of the Caribbean islands (*Back Home Contemplation, I is a Long Memoried Woman*).

Skin-teeth

Not every skin-teeth
is a smile 'Massa'

if you see me smiling
when you pass

if you see me bending
when you ask

Know that I smile
know that I bend

only the better
to rise and strike
again

Grace Nichols from *I is a Long Memoried Woman*

TEXT 4
P.B. Shelley (1792–1822) was one of the second generation of Romantic poets: he, too, was committed to liberty for the individual and supported the cause of the people. This poem was written in 1819, the year of the Peterloo Massacre, when Government troops opened fire on a peaceful crowd gathered in St Peter's Fields to hear a speaker on political reform. Viscount Castlereagh and Viscount Sidmouth were both leading members of the Government at the time. During the same period there was an active parliamentary campaign being waged to abolish slavery.

Similes for Two Political Characters of 1819

As from their ancestral oak
    Two empty ravens wind their clarion,
Yell by yell, and croak by croak,
When they scent the noonday smoke
    Of fresh human carrion: –

As two gibbering night-birds flit
    From their bowers of deadly yew
Through the night to frighten it –
When the moon is in a fit,
    And the stars are none, or few: –

As a shark and dogfish wait
   Under an Atlantic isle
For the Negro-ship, whose freight
Is the theme of their debate,
   Wrinkling their red gills the while –

Are ye – two vultures sick for battle,
   Two scorpions under one wet stone,
Two bloodless wolves whose dry throats rattle,
Two crows perched on the murrained cattle,
   Two vipers tangled into one.

Part 3: Writing about Context: a Methodology

The purpose of this final section is to draw together all we have observed and learnt about context in the last two chapters, and to establish a methodology or strategy which we can use in relation to any text. We are now familiar with the concepts of *readerly* and *writerly* texts, of *reading position* and *writing position*, of the *author–text–reader* dynamic, and of the complex world, past and present, which surrounds and influences the creative process, covertly or overtly. We shall look at two possible strategies.

a Interrogating the text

One simple strategy which is immediately helpful is the concept of *interrogating* a text. Although the word interrogation has some politically negative connotations, the idea of vigorously 'asking questions' of a text rather than simply 'looking at/reading' it, empowers the reader/questioner, because reading a text becomes an *interactive*, not a passive process. As we saw in Chapter 1, texts come alive when they are read, and the more active the reading the better – so why not interrogate them?

But what sort of questions should we ask? The obvious question 'What is the text about?' can only be the starting point for us, since the focus of the entire book is on the *context of text*. More specifically context-oriented questions will be 'Who wrote it?' 'For what audience?' 'When was it written?' 'What was happening in the world when it was written?' The answers to these questions will certainly help our understanding of the context of a text, but in a rather unstructured, even random way.

b Contexts and texts

We need a more systematic and structured methodology, and Rob Pope's four descriptions of context provide a helpful starting point. He differentiates between: *context meaning immediate situation; context meaning larger cultural frame of reference; contexts of (re)production;* and *contexts of reception* (*The English Studies Book* (1998) page 235). To these four we can add a fifth, *context of text*. Let's see whether we can construct a methodology on the basis of these five definitions of context. What we are seeking is an accessible model for looking 'through, round and beyond' a text.

THE MODEL

context meaning immediate situation: *who* is reading the text and from what position? *How* are they reading it and *why*? What *other* readings are currently possible?

contexts of reception: *who* read the text in the past and from what position? *How* did they read it? What *other* readings were possible at that time?

contexts of production: *who* is [was] the author or *producer* of the text? Even if the author is unknown, it remains possible to attempt some of the next questions. *How* and *why* was it written? What is [was] the author's *position* in relation to the text? Has it a significant *publishing history*?

context meaning larger cultural frame of reference: the social, historical, political and cultural environment [past or present] in which the *author produced the text*, and the *readers read the text*.

context of text: what is the *genre*? What is the text *about*? Does it reflect the *writer's individual* and *social experience*? Does it appeal to the *reader's individual* and *social experience*? What literary *influences* or *models* are reflected in the text?

These definitions/descriptors/sets of questions can be applied to **any text at any time in any order**. We'll try out the model on a 'real text' and see how it works, selecting a short, accessible text for the first try-out.

WORKED EXAMPLE

My Father's Father's Father

In this city I have aged thousands of years
I am older than the oldest tree in the world.

There are homes here for ancient holy cows
but none for old people, nowhere for me to go.

It is good that like the cows I am prepared
to wander the lanes and alleyways.

I was here before my father's father's father –
I think I can identify him, rising upwards

like K2 on an early relief map of India.
He is so old his skin is flaking like leaves,

his hair is soft as dust. I take his arm,
tell him who I am, then we are old together.

We vow to bathe ourselves everyday although
we are so old, because like the city

we are hanging by a tough thread
and dead-looking trees

have brilliant purple flowers.

Moniza Alvi *Carrying my Wife* (2000)

context of text: poem, in free verse, about old age and renewal in India: poetic voice a younger member of family, gender unclear.

context meaning immediate situation: the poem is being read by the readers of this book, students of A Level literature, as part of an academic investigation into literary context; they are probably male and female, and most will between aged between 16– 20; they are reading for meaning but aware of other contextual possibilities.

contexts of reception: readers with knowledge of Indian culture will have different experience to bring to the poem: European readers will be learning new perspectives on the experience of being old.

context of production: the poet is a twentieth-century woman who writes in English about Indian life; we have a strong sense of how much her family means to her, and the poem is not literally timebound, but covers a range of generations: the poet enters into the experience of age changing gender and persona. The poetic tone varies from regretful to ironic, even humorous.

context meaning larger cultural frame of reference: the poem evokes the Indian world by alluding to religion ('holy cows'), the physical environment (simile referring to the Himalayan mountain K2), the actual appearance of the old man, and the richness of the exotic purple flowers which are both real and symbolic. Religious and social customs are communicated indirectly ('We vow to bathe ourselves').

ADDITIONAL PRACTICE TEXTS (FOR APPLYING THE 'FIVE CONTEXTS' MODEL)

Waiting Gentlewoman

If daddy had known the setup,
I'm absolutely positive, he'd never
Have let me come. Honestly,
The whole thing's too gruesome
For words. There's nobody here to talk to
At all. Well, nobody under about ninety,
I mean. All the possible men have buggered
Off to the other side, and the rest,
Poor old dears, they'd have buggered off

Too, if their poor old legs would have
Carried them. HM's a super person, of course,
But she's a bit seedy just now,
Quite different from how marvellous she was
At the Coronation. And this doctor they've got in –
Well, he's only an ordinary little GP,
With a very odd accent, and even I
Can see that what HM needs is
A real psychiatrist. I mean, all this
About *blood*, and *washing.* Definitely Freudian.
As for Himself, we, definitely
Not my type. Daddy's got this thing
About self-made men, of course, that's why
He was keen for me to come. But I think
He's gruesome. What HM sees in him
I cannot imagine. *And* he talks to himself.
That's so rude, I always think.
I hope Daddy comes for me soon.

U.A. Fanthorpe *Selected Poems* (1986)

Monday, January 13, 1986. Victor Wilcox lies awake, in the dark bedroom, waiting for his quartz alarm clock to bleep. It is set to do this at 6.45. How long he has to wait he doesn't know. He could easily find out by groping for the clock, lifting it to his line of vision, and pressing the button that illuminates the digital display. But he would rather not know. Supposing it is only six o'clock? Or even five? It could be five. Whatever it is, he won't be able to get to sleep again. This has become a regular occurrence lately: lying awake in the dark, waiting for the alarm to bleep, worrying.

Worries streak towards him like enemy spaceships in one of Gary's video games. He flinches, dodges, zaps them with instant solutions, but the assault is endless: the Avco account, the Rawlinson account, the price of pig-iron. The value of the pound, the competition from Foundrax, the incompetence of his Marketing Director, the persistent breakdowns of the core blowers, the vandalizing of the toilets in the fettling shop, the pressure from his divisional boss, last month's accounts, the quarterly forecast, the annual review . . .

David Lodge *Nice Work* (1988)

Summary

In this chapter we have investigated the role of the author in some detail, including some theoretical approaches. We have explored the question of the 'death of the author', and learnt to distinguish between 'readerly' and 'writerly' texts. Next we looked at context from the writer's position, both as an individual and as part of society. In the final section we have established a set of strategies which should enable us to address the problems of context that different historical and literary periods present to readers.

4 Context of Texts: From Chaucer to the Glorious Revolution

TIMELINE

Date	Event	Dynasty/Monarch
1350	Black Death War with France since **1337** Bible translated into English: *The Canterbury Tales*	**Plantagenet** Edward III d. 1377 Richard II d. 1399
1400	War with France continues (100 Years War)	**Lancaster** Henry IV d. 1413 Henry V d. 1422 Henry VI d. 1461
1450	Civil War – War of Roses between Lancaster and York dynasties Copernicus discovers earth revolves round sun Columbus lands in America	**York** Edward IV d. 1470 Edward V d. 1483 Richard III d. 1485
1500	Protestant Reformation spreads throughout Europe to England: Henry VIII breaks with Rome: Poor Laws force beggary on former farmers: monasteries dissolved. Weaving industry develops	**Tudor** Henry VI d. 1509 Henry VIII d. 1547
1550	British trade in Slaves (**1562**): Sir Francis Drake sails round world. Puritanism becomes established. Spanish Armada defeated (**1588**): Execution of Mary Queen of Scots (**1587**)	Edward VI d. 1553 Mary I d. 1558 Elizabeth I d. 1603
1600	Settlement in New England (**1620**): East India company founded Rise of Puritanism War between Royalists and Puritans (Civil War) King Charles I executed	**Stuart** James I and VI d. 1625 Charles I d. 1649 THE COMMONWEALTH to 1660
1650	Cromwell becomes Protector (**1653–1658**) Monarchy restored (**1660**): Establishment of Royal Society **1665** Great Plague of London **1666** Great Fire of London **1667** Milton's *Paradise Lost* **1688** Glorious Revolution	Charles II d. 1685 James II abdicated 1688 Mary II and William III d. 1694, 1702
1700	War of Spanish succession (**1701**) Battle of Blenheim (**1704**)	Anne d. 1714

Contextualising ourselves!

One of the problems faced by most people when reading 'early texts' is that our knowledge of English history, never mind English literary history is (to put it mildly) *sketchy*! There are many reasons for this, ranging from the fact that most history is learnt in primary school, to the popularity of modern history study at GCSE and A Level, plus a vague feeling that it's all too long ago and difficult to remember and we don't really need it today, do we?... Faced with this kind of problem, how on earth do we deal with the *context* dimension of any early texts we're asked to study, either as whole texts or in extract form? The answer has to be a willingness to apply the imagination *retrospectively*, together with a willingness to memorise a few key events, people and ideas which 'changed the world' at the time these Early Modern writers were at work. As always, we need to try to view texts through the imagined eyes of the original audience as well as from our position today: we also need to try to look through the eyes of the writer, and to see the text within the context of his or her individual and social experience, as far as we can discover it.

The historical period this chapter will focus on covers three centuries – a short period in terms of the history of human beings, but a long time within the narrower framework of Western literary achievement. Note that at this time *literature* simply meant 'learned writings', and had no direct links with the imagination – an association not to be made, in fact, until the nineteenth century. Note too that the writers in English from this period we have chosen to explore (and in this respect we are limited by the examination boards' requirement that we study texts written originally in English) are predominantly male (for reasons we shall discuss later), though we shall look at some women's writing too. They range from a late fourteenth-century poet like Geoffrey Chaucer, (*The Canterbury Tales*) to storytellers like the fifteenth-century Thomas Malory (*Morte D'Arthur*); from sixteenth-century poets and dramatists like John Skelton, Sir Philip Sidney, Christopher Marlowe and William Shakespeare, to seventeenth-century playwrights like Aphra Behn and William Wycherley and poets like George Herbert and Margaret Cavendish. You will see that this range covers a variety of genres, and more will be included (such as travel writing, biography and autobiography).

Writers and readers

How shall we manage all this? The first thing to do is to try and imagine what life was like for writers throughout this period. By definition they would be well-educated, probably able to read Latin (the language of the old Roman Empire, used across Europe as a *lingua franca* in intellectual, diplomatic, legal and cultural circles), and quite possibly fluent in other European languages like French, German or Spanish. Although not necessarily wealthy themselves, the fact of literacy at a high level suggests enough money must have been available to finance their education, either via their own family or through some charitable institution (i.e. the old 'grammar schools'). The profession of writer was probably as hard then as it remains today, and only the most financially secure – or single-minded – would have seen themselves in such terms. Most people had other positions as well, in the diplomatic service, at court, or within the household of some great lord. Women who wrote almost certainly were from privileged backgrounds, where literacy was made available to daughters as well as sons, but where most women's 'careers' would be marriage, child-bearing and household and estate management.

Writing was a privilege, in one sense, because writers tended to be from the middle to upper social classes. *Reading* was also a privilege because the vast majority of people were illiterate (remember the frescos in mediaeval churches, telling the *stories* of the Christian gospel to an illiterate congregation). A few educational opportunities were available to the most able boys (perhaps recognised by the local clergyman or lord of the manor), but for the lower classes education was virtually impossible. However, for the middle classes (merchants, tradesmen, landowners on a small scale, artisans) literacy was increasing and continued to increase throughout the four centuries we are investigating. Even so, books remained extremely expensive, from the late fifteenth-century introduction of the printing press to England (by William Caxton) onwards. However, *knowledge* of books would also have been encouraged by the well-established practice of reading texts aloud in small groups (family, friends, members of the household, courtiers etc.). (Remember too that until the fourteenth century even if you were born an English speaker, your *education* would be in the medium of French, the language of the Norman Conquest, spoken by everyone who had, or aspired to social or political power!)

Social and political change

You need to imagine that as the three centuries covered in this chapter passed, gradual changes affected writers and readers. To do this, we have included a short timeline showing major events and their implications for people living at the time (see page 56). You will notice that the horror of civil war happened not once, but twice, with families divided against each other each time. Similarly, battles raged across the country in the fifteenth-century power struggle between the York and Lancastrian dynasties, as well as wars with Scotland. Religious disputes led to further suffering, war, martyrdoms and the burning of witches, as the Protestant Reformation became more and more powerful. Internationally, the Hundred Years' War against France in the fourteenth and fifteenth centuries was replaced by war with Spain in the sixteenth century. Poverty spread widely as arable farming was replaced by pasture lands, producing wealth for some and reducing many to the workhouse. Disease and death were always near; the first outbreak of bubonic plague was the Black Death of 1348 which became endemic. The next terrible outbreak was the Great Plague of London in 1665. As geographical knowledge developed, colonialism began, with a concurrent development of the slave trade; it even began in our own backyard in 1609, when 12,000 English and Scots chose to settle in Ulster.

Learning and Power

In contrast, great scientific discoveries emerged as well as new technologies. The growth of humanism led to the revival of classical learning, which spread like wildfire through the capitals of Europe, producing great art and architecture, literature and music. Human beings at all levels of society were dominated less by the Church, and more by economics. Writers flourished and had a great deal to say both about their world and about themselves. Yet the poor remained illiterate and vulnerable with high mortality rates, whilst the rich continued their power-struggles in the cause of further wealth acquisition. Gender studies tell us that women's power depended on birth and rank, often enhanced at all levels of society by widowhood, which provided economic independence. Bess of Hardwick, Countess of Shrewsbury and Lady Anne Clifford are fine examples of this. In other respects, political, social and economic power remained in the hands of men.

ACTIVITY 28

Look up the following key people and events (try encyclopedias and/or the Internet) and make brief notes on each.

Present *one* individual or event you find especially interesting to your group.

Black Death
Paston family
Margery Kempe
Copernicus
Martin Luther
Anne Boleyn
Sir Philip Sidney
Lady Anne Clifford
Galileo
Lucy Hutchinson
Margaret Cavendish, Duchess of Newcastle
Gunpowder Plot
Great Fire of London

Having – we hope – developed some sense of the way people at all levels of society lived in our chosen period, we shall now look at some selected texts and examine them, using the model of 'contextual analysis' we described in the concluding section of the previous chapter. It's probably worth saying at this point that the historical scene-setting will be different in focus as well as (obviously) in content in each of the next two chapters, and that a simple rule of thumb to follow in each chapter is to *expect things to be different*. The only thing to be the same in each is the chapter organisation. After the timeline and introductory material, we shall use *genre* as a way of organising the exemplar materials, starting with *poetry*, then *fictional prose*, *drama* and *non-fictional prose*. Another important point to note is that in different genre extracts we shall *foreground* different aspects, in order to avoid repetition.

Part 1: Contextualising Poetry

a Geoffrey Chaucer (c. 1343–1400)

The extract below is from the *General Prologue* to *The Canterbury Tales* by Geoffrey Chaucer, written between 1387–1392 by a man who was familiar with court and literary circles, and who had himself travelled extensively both abroad and at home, often on royal or diplomatic business. The *General Prologue* introduces the pilgrims who are making à pilgrimage to the shrine of St Thomas à Beckett at Canterbury, and who all have their own reasons for setting off from London on this expedition, some spiritual, some less so. The Wife of Bath, the Prioress and her accompanying nun are the only women on the pilgrimage. Each of the pilgrims agrees to tell a story on the way, to entertain the company and enliven the journey. (The Wife of Bath's Tale is about a young knight who has committed an act of rape, and is sent by the queen on a year's quest to discover what women most desire. If he fails, he will die.)

But before the storytelling starts, we are introduced to all the pilgrims, who are twenty-seven in number, including Chaucer himself, as 'narrator'. The Wife of Bath is the nineteenth pilgrim.

From General Prologue to The Canterbury Tales

A good Wif was ther of biside Bath,
But she was somdel deef, and that was scathe.
Of clooth-makyng she hadde swiche an haunt,
She passed them of Ypres and of Gaunt.
In al the parisshe wif ne was ther noon
That to the offrynge bifore hire sholde goon;
And if ther dide, certeyn so wroothe was she,
That she was out of all charitee.
Her coverchiefs ful fyne were of ground;
I dorste swere they weyeden ten pound
That on a Sonday weren upon hir heed.
Hir hosen were of fyne scarlet reed,
Ful streite yteyd, and shoes ful moyste and newe.
Boold was hir face, and fair, and reed of hewe.
She was a worthy womman al hir lyve:
Housbondes at chirche dore she hadde fyve,
Withouten oother compaignye inn youthe, –
But therof nedeth nat to speke as nowthe.
... Gat-tothed was she, soothly for to seye.
Upon an amblere esily she sat,
Ywimpled wel, and on hir heed an hat
As brood as is a bokeler or a targe;
A foot-mantel about hir hipes large,
And on hir feet a paire of spores sharpe.
In felaweshipe wel could she laugh and carpe.
Of remedies of love she knew per chaunce,
For she koude of that art the olde daunce.

Context of text: the passage on the previous page describes the 'larger-than-life' Wife of Bath in blank verse, with the narrator making passing comments addressed directly to the audience about her ('and that was scathe', 'I dorste swere', 'but thereof nedeth nat to speke as nowth'). The genre is a familiar mediaeval pattern – a group of different stories with the same or different narrators (we have similar groupings today – cf Armisted Maupin's California tales, or even the self-contained episodes of television series like *Frasier* or *Sex and the City*).

The Wife of Bath from her description is a woman of imposing appearance, both in physique and dress. We can make some guesses about her character: sensual (implied by reference to husbands and lovers); proud and status-conscious (wants to present the offering first); adventurous (pilgrimages across Europe); skilled in her business (comparison with European master-weavers); wealthy but provincial (best quality clothes and shoes, but not in the height of fashion); good-humoured but quick-tempered (laughs and chats in company); sophisticated in affairs of the heart.

Context of immediate situation including other readings: a twenty-first-century reader, having worked through the language problem, should have come to the sort of conclusions described above. As a portrait of a woman, the type is reasonably familiar, but the value systems and social experiences of her world are far from ours.

As modern post-feminist readers we may be attracted by the Wife's evident independence and frank sensuality. The power and economic status conferred on her by widowhood contradicts stereotypes about women in the late Middle Ages. Her robust attitude to sex and sexuality might also appeal to contemporary post-Freudian readers.

Context of reception: Chaucer's audience would be familiar with the social world of clothmaking in a small town in the West of England (a good 4–5 day's journey from London). They would recognise the references to Jerusalem, Rome etc. as places of pilgrimage for the wealthy. Obviously her old-fashioned dress would be familiar, and they would pick up Chaucer's hints about her lusty nature ('gat-tothed' and 'scarlet hosen'). In what circumstances the text would have been read we can't be sure. It may have been passed round in manuscript or read aloud. Almost certainly the audience would be educated, perhaps members of the court or of a noble household.

Context of production: solid knowledge about Chaucer's life and experience is variable, although we know that he was the son of a vintner (wine merchant) and was employed both in a noble household and on the King's business. Well travelled at home and abroad, his satiric portrait of late medieval society in *The Canterbury Tales* may be partly based on real people he encountered, partly on character stereotypes, and partly invented. As writer or producer of the text, Chaucer adopts a dual role as both writer and participant, through his *alter ego* Chaucer the pilgrim (who accompanies the company on its slow journey to Canterbury). Through his point of view, Chaucer can make seemingly innocent, but actually sharply ironic comments about the other pilgrims (e.g. 'Withouten oother compaignie in youthe'!).

Context of wider frame of reference: the gap between Chaucer's time and today is over 600 years! Obviously the political, social, economic, cultural and religious contexts are hugely different. Yet once the difficulty with the language is overcome, and readers learn a little about social and religious practices, most twentieth and twenty-first-century readers of Chaucer can make viable links between his world and their own, enjoying his ironic humour as well as his anger with the hypocrites and villains of the late fourteenth century.

b Sir Thomas Wyatt (1503–1542)

Diplomat, poet and courtier, Wyatt's fortunes rose and fell depending on his position in the king's favour. Although he was imprisoned on several occasions (once for his earlier relationship with Anne Boleyn) he survived to die of fever.

Whoso lists hunt, I know where is an hind,
　But as for me – alas, I may no more.
　The vain travail hath wearied me so sore,
　I am of them that farthest cometh behind.
Yet may I, by no means, my wearied mind
　Draw from the deer; but as she fleeth afore
　Fainting I follow. I leave off therefore,
　Since in a net I seek to hold the wind.
Who list her hunt, I put him out of doubt,
　As well as I, may spend his time in vain.
　And graven with diamonds in letters plain
There is written, her fair neck round about:
　Noli me tangere, for Caesar's I am,
　And wild for to hold, though I seem tame.

Context of text: the poem is a sonnet based on the Petrarchan model (*abba, abba, cddc, ee*), popular in the sixteenth century. What is it about? It seems that the poet is attempting to capture a deer; not only is he unsuccessful in the chase and withdraws, but he also discovers that she belongs to someone as powerful as a Roman emperor.

ACTIVITY 29

When you have read the historical facts listed below, answer the following questions:

a How do you interpret the poem, literally or metaphorically – or both?
b Give specific textual references to support your points.
c What have you discovered about the **context of reference**?

■ Wyatt held a range of diplomatic posts in the court of Henry VIII.
■ He travelled in Italy, imitated and translated the Italian poet Petrarch's work into English.

■ He spent much of his time at court.
■ *Noli me tangere quia Caesaris sum* (Latin) was the inscription on the collar of Caesar's deer so huntsmen would avoid them.
■ He dedicated a translation from the French to Queen Catherine of Aragon whilst Henry was in the process of divorcing her.
■ He had been an intimate acquaintance of Anne Boleyn, Henry VIII's second wife.
■ Renaissance poets still used some of the traditions of *courtly love*, including the stereotypical suffering experienced by one or both lovers.

In relation to the **context of production** and **context of reception** the *audience* for this sonnet would be the court and other cultivated circles. Readers would be familiar with the traditions Wyatt worked with, and might well 'read' the sub-text. Undoubtedly Wyatt as *producer* of the text chose to disguise the true subject of the poem for reasons of personal safety. Are any **other readings** (**context of immediate situation**) possible today? We may see this as a deliberately ambiguous poem, despite its conventional beginning as a Petrarchan imitation, and may admire it for its deviation. To what extent does it *endorse* conventional gender values?

c George Herbert (1593–1633)

Herbert came from an Anglo-Welsh aristocratic family, and was a successful poet, university orator and Member of Parliament until about 1624, when he decided to enter the church, ultimately becoming a country parson near Salisbury.

The Collar

I struck the board, and cried, No more.
      I will abroad.
  What? shall I ever sigh and pine?
My lines and life are free; free as the road,
   Loose as the wind, as large as store.
      Shall I be still in suit?
  Have I no harvest but a thorn
  To let me blood, and not restore
  What I have lost with cordial fruit?
     Sure there was wine
Before my sighs did dry it; there was corn
    Before my tears did drown it.
  Is the year only lost to me?
    Have I no bays to crown it?
No flowers, no garlands gay? All blasted?
     All wasted?
  Not so, my heart: but there is fruit,
    And thou hast hands.
  Recover all thy sigh-blown age
On double pleasures: leave thy cold dispute
Of what is fit, and not. Forsake thy cage,
    Thy rope of sands,
Which petty thoughts have made, and made to thee
  Good cable, to enforce and draw
    And be thy law,
  While thou didst wink and would not see.
    Away; take heed
    I will abroad,
Call in thy death's head there: tie up thy fears.
    He that forbears
  To suit and serve his need

>Deserves his load.
>But as I raved and grew more fierce and wild
>   At every word,
>Me thoughts I heard one calling, *Child!*
>   And I replied, *My Lord.*

Who is the audience for this poem? It seems extremely personal – about the writer's wrestling with his vocation or even with God. The audience is the poet himself, and the readers (both seventeenth century and today's) seem to eavesdrop on this disturbing, confrontational and passionate harangue. How on earth can we disentangle the context(s)?

ACTIVITY 30

Read the additional information about Herbert below, and answer the following questions:

a How far does the biographical information help you to understand the emotions revealed in the poem?

b Choose three images which you find particularly effective in communicating the poet's feelings. With a partner, analyse the way each image works.

- Herbert was a Fellow at Cambridge, and moved in high university, court and parliamentary circles.
- At 31 he turned away from his previous life, was ordained, and until his premature death from tuberculosis in his fortieth year 'gained a reputation for humility, energy and charity' in his village parishes.
- He was a Protestant.
- He was associated with the religious community at Little Gidding in Cambridgeshire, which 300 years later gave its name to one of T.S. Eliot's poems *Four Quartets*.
- 'Collar' may be a pun on clerical dress.
- 'Board' can mean table or communion table.
- 'Store' means plenty.
- 'In suit' means in attendance.

Context of text: the poem is in an unusual metrical form – can you suggest what effect this has? In the **context of production** the poem seems autobiographical, *writerly* in its position, with readers distanced (**context of immediate situation**)from the central emotions. The **context of reception** assumes a contemporary readership sympathetic to the poet's religious experience, which would be readily available in 1633, when his poems were published posthumously. In today's more secular age, there would be less understanding amongst readers; even so, the struggle described would be readily recognised. A more likely reading would focus on the poetic language, particularly metaphors. The **context of cultural reference** would be the powerful Protestant movement in England which would lead to the tragedy of the Civil War in 1642.

d Andrew Marvell (1621–1678)

Marvell was a Yorkshireman, famous until relatively recently more for his political astuteness and love of liberty (he was Latin Secretary to Cromwell after Milton) than for his poetry.

Bermudas

Where the remote Bermudas ride
In th'ocean's bosom unespied,
From a small boat that rowed along,
The list'ning winds received this song:
   What should we do but sing his praise
That led us through the wat'ry maze
Unto an isle so long unknown,
And yet far kinder than our own?
Where he the huge sea-monster wracks,
That lift the deep upon their backs,
He lands us on a grassy stage,
Safe from the storms and prelates' rage.
He gave us this eternal spring
Which here enamels everything,
And sends the fowls to us in care,
On daily visits through the air.
He hangs in shades the orange bright,
Like golden lamps in the green night;
And does in the pomegranates close
Jewels more rich than Ormus shows.
He makes the figs our mouths to meet
And throws the melons at our feet . . .
   . . . Thus sung they in the English boat
An holy and a cheerful note,
And all the way, to guide their chime,
With falling oars they kept the time.

Context of text: this *lyric* poem is about the English colonists who fled across the Atlantic to escape religious persecution in the early seventeenth century, and found themselves off the coast of the mid-Atlantic coast island of Bermuda. It is probably an imagined scene, based on the stories Marvell had heard about the island from people who had travelled there. In terms of the **context of reception,** contemporary readers would adopt different positions, depending on their attitude to the colonists seeking religious freedom. However, the poem was not published until 1681, when the Atlantic colonies were well established, and less controversial. Marvell himself wrote the poem when he was 22 and acting as a tutor to Cromwell's ward, perhaps inspired by the travellers' tales he had heard. In his subsequent career he was MP for Hull for 20 years, and wrote political rather than lyric poetry (**context of production**). Today a **different reading** might take a *post-colonial* view, challenging the validity of colonising the Bermudas, of the Eden myth and of the flight from religious persecution.

ACTIVITY 31

Look up the following (using the Internet, encyclopaedias etc.): history of Bermuda, prelate, Ormus, sea-monsters. Using this extra information as you see fit, write an imagined account of the voyagers' arrival on the island of Bermuda based on this extract from Marvell's poem (it could be in the form of a diary entry, letter home or even a narrative).

e Unseen poem

Of Many Worlds in This World

Just like unto a nest of boxes round,
Degrees of sizes within each box are found,
So in this world may many worlds more be,
Thinner, and less, and less still by degree;

Although they are not subject to our sense,
A world may be no bigger than twopence.
Nature is curious, and such work may make
That our dull sense can never find, but scape.
For creatures small as atoms may be there,
If every atom a creature's figure bear.
If four atoms a world can make, then see
What several worlds might in an ear-ring be.
For millions of these atoms may be in
The head of one small, little, single pin.
And if thus small, then ladies well may wear
A world of worlds as pendents in each ear.

ACTIVITY 32

Read the unseen poem through several times, and using the five-context framework, write down under each context heading what you can deduce about it from the evidence of the text. Under the *context of production* the following clues are provided: the poet is female and writing in the mid seventeenth century. You may, for example, note that the poet refers to science and geography as well as to jewellery and pins – under which *context* headings might this information fit?

Part 2: Contextualising Literary Prose

a Sir Thomas Malory (d. 1471)

Malory is rather a mysterious figure, though it's thought that he wrote most of *Morte D'Arthur* as a prisoner, probably in England, possibly in France.

From Le Morte D'Arthur

How Arthur by the means of Merlin gat Excalibur his sword of the Lady of the Lake

Right so the king and he departed, and went unto a hermit that was a good man and a great leech. So the hermit searched all his wounds and gave him good salves; so the king was there three days, and then were his wounds well amended that he might ride and go, and so departed. And as they rode, Arthur said, I have no sword. No force, said Merlin, hereby is a sword that shall be yours, an I may. So they rode till they came to a lake, the which was a fair water and broad, and in the midst of the lake Arthur was ware of an arm clothed in white samite, that held a fair sword in that hand. Lo! said Merlin, yonder is that sword that I spake of. With that they saw a damosel going upon the lake. What damosel is that? said Arthur. That is the Lady of the Lake, said Merlin; and within that lake is a rock, and therein is as fair a place as any on earth, and richly beseen; and this damosel will come to you anon, and then speak ye fair to her that she will give you that sword. Anon withal came the damosel unto Arthur, and saluted him, and he her again. Damosel, said Arthur, what sword is that, that yonder the arm holdeth above the water? I would it were mine, for I have no sword. Sir Arthur, king, said the damosel, that sword is mine, and if ye will give me a gift when I ask it you, ye shall have it.

Contexts of reception and production: though we know little about Malory's life, we know that he used a wide variety of sources (Welsh, French, Breton, Celtic, Latin and Anglo-Saxon) as the basis for his cycle of Arthurian legends. Fifteenth-century readers would be familiar with stories of King Arthur, the knights of the Round Table and the world of chivalric romance. Modern readers too know many of the stories, possibly learnt at primary school – as well as the parodic versions offered by Monty Python. Arthur himself continues to function as a kind of British hero, traditionally waiting in some hidden secret place (Glastonbury, the Welsh mountains, the Eildon Hills in Scotland) to return when his country needs him. Within the **context of cultural reference** the Arthurian legends have many symbolic associations with chivalry and representations of gender. In *historic* terms the romance was produced at the time of the Wars of the Roses, when England was suffering the ravages of civil war. *Le Morte D'Arthur* tells of many battles, much devastation, and the ultimate departure and death of Arthur – matching, perhaps, the dark mood of the contemporary audience.

ACTIVITY 33

a The Arthurian legends are traditionally called 'romances' (though our current use of the word is rather different). If we use an earlier definition of romance, linking it with fantasy as opposed to 'reality', what would you pick out as 'romantic' features in the passage above?

b How would you 'read' this passage from a feminist position? (You may like to consider what view is taken of the Lady of the Lake by Arthur and Merlin; what is her attitude to them; and what assumptions are implicit about women and status in fifteenth-century society).

b Sir Philip Sidney (1554–86) and Thomas Nashe (c. 1567–1601)

Sidney's legend argues that he was the perfect Renaissance man – soldier, diplomat, poet courtier – whose early death resulted in several famous elegies, including one by Raleigh. He wrote a fine sonnet sequence, *Astrophel and Stella* and the prose romance *Arcadia*. Nashe was a well-known Elizabethan pamphleteer and satirist, who pioneered the 'rogue' or picaresque novel.

From The Countess of Pembroke's Arcadia (1590)

There were hills which garnished their proud heights with stately trees; humble valleys whose base estate seemed comforted with refreshing of silver rivers; meadows enamelled with all sorts of eye-pleasing flowers; thickets, which, being lined with most pleasant shade, were witnessed so to by the cheerful deposition of many well-tuned birds; each pasture stored with sheep feeding with sober security ... here a shepherd's boy piping as though he should never be old; there a young shepherdess knitting and withal singing ... As for the houses of the country ... they were all scattered ... yet not so far off as that it barred mutual succour; a show, as it were, of an accompanable solitude and of a civil wildness.

From The Unfortunate Traveller or The Life of Jack Wilton (1594)

About the time that the terror of the world and fever quartane of the French, Henry the Eight ... advanced his standard against the two hundred and fifty towers of Turney [Tournai] and Turwin [Terouanne] ... I, Jack Wilton, a gentleman at least, was a certain kind of appendix or page, belonging or appertaining in or unto the confines of the English Court; where what my credit was, a number of my creditors that I cozened [tricked] can testify ... Be it known to as many as will pay money enough to peruse my story, that I followed the Court or the camp, or the camp or the Court ... There did I (soft, let me drink before I go any further) reign King of the Cans and Black-jacks, Prince of the Pigmies, County Palatine of Clean Straw and Provant [food], and to conclude, Lord High Regent of Rashers of the Coals and Red-herring Cobs [fish-heads].

These two extracts from early fiction were published within four years of each other (**context of cultural frame of reference**), and must have been intended for virtually the same audience (**context of reception**). The *Arcadia* extract reflects the courtly world of Elizabethan pastoral romance, in which the noble heroes experience many adventures before being united with their true loves. *The Unfortunate Traveller* extract prepares the reader for the low life adventures of Jack Wilton, gentleman-trickster, card-playing courtier and soldier *(***context of text***)*. The appeal of each text is very different, and though both might have been enjoyed by members of the court, the tone of one is poetic, scholarly, coolly aristocratic, whilst the other is exaggerated and comically direct. The **contexts of production** are obviously different, since despite the fact that Sidney and Nashe died at a similar age, in their early thirties, they are writers with widely different social experience, who use different literary models and have differing intentions.

ACTIVITY 34

a What kind of problems might a twenty-first century reader have with these texts? What aspects might appeal to a contemporary reader? Give reasons for your comments.

b What specific differences in language do you find between the two texts?

c Unseen prose

It is too little to call man a little world; except God, man is a diminutive to nothing. Man consists of more pieces, more parts than the world; than the world doth, nay than the world is. And if those pieces were extended and stretched out in man as they are in the world, man would be the giant and the world the dwarf; the world but the map, and the man the world. If all the veins in our bodies were extended to rivers, and all the sinews to veins of mines, and all the muscles that lie upon one another to hills, and all the bones to quarries of stones, and all the other pieces to the proportion of those which correspond to them in the world, the air would be too little for this orb of man to move in, the firmament would be but enough for this star. For as the whole world hath nothing to which something in man does not answer, so hath man many pieces of which the whole world hath no representation.

ACTIVITY 35

Apply the *five context framework* to the text above. In relation to the *context of production* the author is a seventeenth-century churchman; the genre (*context of text*) is a meditation.

Part 3: Contextualising Drama

a Christopher Marlowe (1564–1593)

A contemporary of Shakespeare, Marlowe was almost certainly involved in espionage as well as being an admired poet and dramatist. His most famous plays include *Dr Faustus* and *Tamburlaine*. He had a reputation for violence, and was actually killed during a tavern quarrel.

From Edward the Second Act V Scene 1

Enter the King, Leicester, *with the* Bishop of Winchester *and* Trussel.
Edward Leicester, if gentle words might comfort me,
Thy speeches long ago had eased my sorrows,
For kind and loving hast thou always been.
The griefs of private men are soon allayed
But not of kings; the forest deer being struck
Runs to an herb that closeth up the wounds
But when the imperial lion's flesh is gored
He rends and tears it with his wrathful paw
[And] highly scorning that the lowly earth
Should drink his blood, mounts up into the air;
And so it fares with me, whose dauntless mind
The ambitious Mortimer would seek to curb
And that unnatural queen, false Isabel,
That thus hath pent and mewed me in a prison;
... But when I call to mind I am a king,
Methinks I should revenge me of the wrongs
That Mortimer and Isabel have done.
But what are kings when regiment is gone
But perfect shadows in a sunshine day?
My nobles rule, I bear the name of king;

I wear the crown but am controlled by them,
By Mortimer and my unconstant queen,
Who spots my nuptial bed with infamy
Whilst I am lodged within this cave of care,
Where sorrow at my elbow still attends ...
But tell me, must I now resign my crown
To make usurping Mortimer a king?

To understand the context of drama texts is significantly different from considering the context of prose or poetry texts. A further dimension is involved, in that plays are primarily intended to be *heard and seen*, not read. Studying plays simply as *written* texts probably evolved in the late nineteenth century, with the rise of English studies as a university subject. More recently, the importance of considering *performance* when studying a play has been recognised in school, college and university English teaching. So when we consider the **contexts** of these extracts from plays, we must always bear in mind the *performance aspects*.

Context of text: the subject of Marlowe's play *Edward the Second* is the story of the king whose passion for his favourite Gaveston led him to forget his royal duties and responsibilities. The nobles revolted against him, their leader being Mortimer, the queen's lover. Edward was imprisoned, and in this scene is required to hand over the crown itself. Performed in 1592 (**context of reception**), the play would have appealed to contemporary audiences with its focus on the tragic downfall of three historic figures – Edward, Mortimer and Gaveston, and the gruesome murder of Edward himself, played out in the intimate setting of the Elizabethan playhouse. The **context of cultural frame of reference** would include: the turbulent political times both nationally and internationally; the status of majesty and kingship; the succession; court intrigue and royal favourites; the corruption of power. In the **context of immediate situation** the play would be read as an indictment of private passion over public duty. **Other readings** today take a very different perspective on monarchy and kingship, its rights and responsibilities. In terms of *performance* today, a basic understanding of Elizabethan theatre and performance techniques is necessary, even if a 'contemporary' slant is taken on the play.

ACTIVITY 36

a Find out more about the short, violent life of Christopher Marlowe (**context of production**), using your school or college library and the Internet.

b Check that you have a clear understanding of the physical structure of an Elizabethan theatre (try the Globe Theatre website www.shakespeare-globe.org).

c How does the information you have acquired help you to understand the extract above, and support your understanding of the *context of production*?

b) Aphra Behn (1640–1689)

Aphra Behn was a remarkable woman whose skills as a writer and dramatist had been long forgotten until Virginia Woolf wrote admiringly of her in *A Room of her Own* (1928). Her work is now much better known, and her plays quite often performed.

From The Rover (1677) Act 1 Scene 1

Naples, in Carnival time. Enter Florinda, Valeria and Hellena (sisters).

Florinda What an impertinent thing is a young girl bred in a nunnery! How full of questions! Prithee no more, Hellena; I have told thee more than thou understand'st already.

Hellena The more's my grief. I would fain know as much as you, which makes me so inquisitive; nor is't enough I know you're a lover, unless you tell me too who 'tis you sigh for.

Florinda When you're a lover I'll think you fit for a secret of that nature.

Hellena 'Tis true, I never was a lover yet, but I begin to have a shrewd guess what 'tis to be so, and fancy it very pretty to sigh, and sing, and blush, and wish, and dream and wish, and long and wish to see the man, and when I do, look pale and tremble, just as you did when my brother brought home the fine English colonel to see you. What do you call him? Don Belvile?

Florinda Fie, Hellena.

Hellena That blush betrays you. I am sure 'tis so. Or is it Don Antonio the Viceroy's son? Or perhaps the rich old Don Vincentio, whom my father designs you for a husband? Why do you blush again?

Florinda With indignation; and how near soever my father thinks I am to marrying that hated object, I shall let him see I understand better what's due to my beauty, birth and fortune, and more to my soul, than to obey those unjust commands.

Hellena Now hang me, if I don't love you for that dear disobedience. I love mischief strangely, as most of our sex do who are come to love nothing else. But tell me, dear Florinda, don't you love that fine *Anglese* [Englishman]? For I vow, next to loving him myself, 'twill please me most that you do so, for he is so gay and so handsome.

Florinda Hellena, a maid designed for a nun ought not to be so curious in a discourse of love.

Hellena And dost thou think that ever I'll be a nun? Or at least till I'm so old I'm fit for nothing else? Faith no, sister; and that which makes me long to know whether you love Belvile, is because he has some mad companion or other that will spoil my devotion. Nay, I'm resolved to provide myself this Carnival, if there be e'er a handsome proper fellow of my humour above ground, though I ask first.

ACTIVITY 37

Use the following information to identify as many as possible *contexts* for this extract.

- Title page of first edition of play:

THE ROVER:
OR the Banish't Cavaliers.

A COMEDY: ACTED AT
His Royal Highness
THE Duke's Theatre.

Written by
Mrs. A. Behn.

Licensed July 2d.1677.

- *The Rover* was an immediate success.
- During the Civil War, many Cavaliers fled England to live in exile abroad. Many became mercenary soldiers, with no responsibilities or ties, and a reputation for wild living. They returned to England after the restoration of Charles II to the throne.
- Aphra Behn was the first of a group of female playwrights in the Restoration period. (Others include Mary Pix and Susannah Centlivre.)
- After returning from a family visit to Surinam in 1663, Aphra married a Dutch merchant, Behn, in the same year. Widowed after two years of marriage, she was then forced to earn her living by writing.
- She was a spy in Antwerp for Charles II in 1666 before she began writing plays. Her earliest known writings are encoded intelligence reports. She wrote a dozen more plays after *The Rover*, as well as a novel, *Orinooko, or the History of the Royal Slave*, based on her observation of the slave trade in Surinam.
- Behn held strong views on female equality; her position has been described as 'broad, democratic and even-handed'. Unfortunately her contemporary literary reputation only lasted 50 years after her death, after which her work was deliberately kept out of print as 'unfeminine'. One critic suggests that 'her real offence seems to have been the even-handedness of her comedy, where men are never ridiculed any less than women'.
- Her work has recently been the subject of much interest, and her plays revived, as a result of the feminist movement and the consequent reprinting of 'lost' texts by women.
- The extract above is the opening scene of the play and establishes character, time and setting, as well as preparing us for the plot (Hellena will indeed find 'some mad companion, to 'spoil' her 'devotion' – Willmore, the Rover).

ACTIVITY 38

The unseen passage below is taken from a play performed two years before *The Rover*. Read it carefully and then answer the following questions:

a What differences and similarities do you notice between the *characters* of Hellena and Mrs Pinchwife?

b How does the *dialogue* in each extract show these differences and similarities?

Unseen drama

Mrs Pinchwife Pray, sister, where are the best fields and woods to walk in, in London?

Alithea [aside] A pretty question! [Aloud] Why, sister, Mulberry Gardens and St James's Park; and, for close walks, the New Exchange.

Mrs Pinchwife Pray, sister, tell me why my husband looks so grum here in town, and keeps me up so close, and will not let me go a-walking, nor let me wear my best gown yesterday.

Alithea O, he's jealous, sister.

Mrs Pinchwife Jealous! What's that?

Alithea He's afraid you should love another man.

Mrs Pinchwife How should he be afraid of my loving another man, when he will not let me see any but himself?

Alithea Did he not carry you to a play yesterday?

Mrs Pinchwife Ay; but we sat amongst ugly people. He would not let me come near the gentry, who sat under us, so that I could not see them. He told me, none but naughty women sat under there, who they toused and moused. But I would have ventured, for all that.

Alithea But how did you like the play?

Mrs Pinchwife Indeed I was weary of the play; but I like hugeously the actors. They are the goodliest properest men, sister!

Part 4: Contextualising Non-Literary Prose

Non-literary prose is a wide-ranging category, including a variety of genres, from journalism and essays to travel literature, letters, philosophical or scientific writing, diaries and pamphlets. Determining the contexts of these differing genres is as important as determining the contexts of literary texts, and equally crucial to their proper understanding. In the period covered by this chapter, some interesting non-literary prose texts include the fifteenth-century *Paston Letters*, Richard Hakluyt's *The Principal Navigations, Voyages, Trafiques and Discoveries of the English Nation* (1599), Francis Bacon's scientific writing *The Advancement of Learning* (1605), Lucy Hutchinson's Civil War *Memoirs of the Life of Colonel Hutchinson*, the diaries of Lady Anne Clifford (1603–1676), political pamphlets (e.g. Milton's 1643 *The Doctrine and Discipline of Divorce*), and John Bunyan's *Pilgrim's Progress* (1678). We shall look at two short extracts only, both by women: a pamphlet defending women from sexist criticism and a diary extract.

a Jane Anger (dates unknown)

JANE ANGER her Protection for Women To defend them against the SCANDALOUS REPORTES OF a late Surfeiting Lover, and all other like Venerians that complaine so to bee overcloyed with womens kindnesse (1589)

The desire that every man hath to show his true vein in writing is unspeakable, and their minds so carried away with the manner as no care at all is had of the matter. They run so into rhetoric as oftentimes they overrun the bounds of their own wits, and go they know not whither. If they have stretched their invention so hard on a last

as it is at a stand, there remains but one help, which is, to write of us women.
... And therefore ... their wits whetted and their brains almost broken with botching
[Apollo's] bounty, they fall straight to dispraising and slandering our silly [simple]
sex. ... they suppose that there is not one amongst us who can, or dare, reprove
their slanders and false reproaches. ... They have been so daintily fed with our good
natures that like jades (their stomachs are grown queasy) they surfeit of our
kindness. ... Yet if we bear with their rudeness and be somewhat modestly familiar
with them, they will straight make matter of nothing, blazing abroad that they have
surfeited with love; and then their wits must be shown in telling the manner how.

The rest of the pamphlet argues vigorously against men who slander
women for the very faults they themselves are guilty of, imposing their will
but blaming women. False slander may be a male joke but it can destroy
the life of a woman. The **contexts of reception and immediate situation**
all relate to the gender and gendered position of the audience, and whether
the extract is being read in the late sixteenth or the early twenty-first
century. To the male Elizabethans, accustomed to male-centred texts about
love and the lover's experience, the pamphlet might be disturbing;
Elizabethan women on the other hand might be convinced by the
argument. Modern readers of either gender may be sympathetic with the
predicament described, aware of women's disempowerment at the time of
writing.

The **contexts of production and of cultural frame of reference** are not
easy to disentangle, since the authorship of the text is not certain, and
neither is the gender. It is possible to say, however, that pamphlets by
women were being published at this time, usually on domestic matters, or
religious topics. This pamphlet is less usual, though it is one of several
attacking male representations of women, who had no 'voice' in the public
domain, however active and responsible they might be at home or in
business. The **context of genre** confirms the text's link with the popular
genre of pamphlets, typically dealing with matters of topical or political
interest, and highly rhetorical in style. Jane Anger models her pamphlet on
contemporary examples, making sure that her style is as elegant and her
references as learned as any male pamphleteer's.

b Lady Anne Clifford (1590–1676)

From The Kendal Diary 1650–1675

In the yeare of ower Lorde God in 1665

The 23rd of Februarie in this year between 11 and 12 a clock in the forenoon was my
Grandchild the Ladie Frances Tufton now second daughter to my daughter Thanet
and her deceased Lord, married in the Chappell in Thanet House in Aldersgate Street
at London ... to Mr Henry Drax. Which Grandchild of mine had bin once or twice in
the Low Countries for the cure of Ricketts. But thanks be to God she came now to be
well married.
About the 29th of June in this yeare being St Peter's Day, did our Queene Marie, the
Frenchwoman, Queene Dowager and Mother of our King Charles the second goe out
of Somersett House and out of London Towne ... by easy journies to Dover in Kent.

Her two sonnes, our King Charles and James Duke of York ... all took their leaves of her as she was on shipboard ... from whence she cross'd the seas in one of ye Kinges shippes and landed safely at Calais, and from thence went to Paris.

And in this year 1665 and the beginning of the yeare following, was there a great Plague in the Cittie and suburbs of London, whereof there died for severall weekes together above 8,000 a week, the like whereof was never known in London before. The first day of August this yeare, I had layen 9 monthes and 7 daies over in Brougham Castle in Westmerland in the Chamber where my noble father was borne and my Blessed Mother dyed; did I then remove with all my family out of the said Brougham Castle into my Castle of Appleby in Westmerland. ... and continued to lye in this Appleby Castle till the 10th November followinge, that I removed from hence with my familie into Brough Castle in the same Countie. And.. I now begun to lye in the highest Round Chamber on Clifford's Tower ... and in this Brough Castle did I keepe my Christmas in it, which was the first Christmas I ever kept in the said Castle, nor had any of my Ancestors done it since the yeare 1521 ... it being then burnt down ...

The 22nd of the said November, about one a clock in the afternoon, (to my unspeakable grreife), dyed my dear Grandchild the Ladie Frances Drax ... being then in Labour of her first Childe which was a Sonne of whom she could not be delivered, for the Childe was dead within her a few houres before her owne death. And both when she dyed and was burried did I lye in my owne Chamber in Cliffords Tower in Brough Castle where I heard first of all the sad news of her death, the 6th day of the said December.

Context of text: Lady Anne Clifford was the daughter of two noble Northern families, who spent the first half of her life defending her right as a woman to be her father's heir, whilst dealing with the consequences of two difficult marriages. She finally won her case, and retired to the North, where she spent the rest of her life restoring her castles and lands, protecting her servants, tenants and friends, and regularly entertaining or corresponding with her children and grandchildren. The diaries were described by her as Books of Record, so they were in no sense private. They present the reader with a range of social, historical, political and personal insights into several worlds: the Court (she attended Queen Elizabeth's funeral as a thirteen year old; lived through the execution of Charles I, the Civil War and the restoration of Charles II); the judiciary (her efforts to secure her inheritance were constantly rebuffed); political intrigues affecting her and her family; and the world of estate management.

ACTIVITY 39

The five-context model is less easy to apply to diaries because many are intended only for the eye of the writer. Others, of course (particularly political diaries) are certainly aimed at a public audience.

a What evidence you can find in the extract from Lady Anne Clifford's diary of: *context of production; context of cultural frame of reference; context of immediate situation?*

b What similarities and differences can you identify between the contexts of Lady Anne Clifford's diary and the unseen text on page 76?

Unseen text

Monday, Octob'r. *ye* second, 1704. After three o'clock afternoon, I begun my journey from Boston to New-Haven; being about two Hundred Mile . . .

Wednesday, Octob'r 4th. About four in the morning, we set out for Kingston (for so was the Town called) with a french Doctor in our company. Hee and *ye* Post put on very furiously, so that I could not keep up with them, only as now and then they'd stop till they see mee. This Rode was poorly furnished *wth* accommodations for Travellers, so that we were forced to ride 22 miles by the post's account, but neerer thirty by mine, before wee could bait so much as our Horses, *wch* I exceedingly complained of. But the post encourag'd mee, saying we should be well accommodated anon at mr. Devills, a few miles further. But I questioned whether we ought to go to the Devil to be helpt out of affliction. However, like the rest of Deluded souls that post to *ye* infernal denn, Wee made all posible speed to this Devil's Habitation; where alliting, I full assurance of good accommodation, wee were going in. But meeting his two daughters, as I suposed twins, they so neerly resembled each other, both in features and habit, and lookt as old as the Divel, and quite as Ugly, Wee desired entertainm't, but could hardly get a word out of 'um, till with our Importunity . . . they called the old Sophister, who was as sparing of his words as his daughters had bin, and no, or none, was the reply's hee made us to our demands. Hee differed only from the old fellow in to'other Country: hee let us depart.

Summary

In this chapter we have put into practice the model of contextual analysis described at the end of Chapter 3, and looked at three major literary genres and some non-literary texts. We have provided an unseen passage at the end of each section to enable you to practice contextual analysis, with suggested approaches for each. In the next chapter we shall be covering a shorter period historically, but as you will see, new times bring new texts and new contexts.

5 Context of Texts: From Queen Anne to Queen Victoria

TIMELINE

Date	Event	Dynasty/Monarch
1700	Act of Succession (**1706**) Union of England and Scotland (**1707**) 1st Jacobite Rebellion (**1715**) South Sea Bubble (**1720**) 2nd Jacobite Rebellion (**1745**) Battle of Culloden (**1746**)	**Hanover** George I d. 1727 George II d. 1760
1750	Johnson's Dictionary (**1755**) Capture of Quebec (**1755**) Boston Tea Party (**1773**) War of American Independence Declaration of Independence (**1776**): Penal colonies established in Australia (**1788**) French Revolution (**1789**) Execution of Louis XVI War with France	George III d. 1820
1800	Act of Union Britain and Ireland (**1801**) End of British slave trade (**1802**) Napoleon crowned Emperor Battle of Trafalgar (**1805**) Battle of Waterloo (**1815**) Peterloo Massacre (**1819**) Famine in Ireland (**1821**) Reform Act (**1832**) Slavery abolished in British Empire (**1834**) Chartist Riots (**1839**) Revolution in France and across Europe (**1848**)	George IV d. 1830 William IV d. 1837 Victoria d. 1901
1850	Communist Manifesto by Marx and Engels Great Exhibition (**1851**) Crimean War (**1854–56**) Indian Mutiny (**1858**) American Civil War (**1860–1865**) Canada given self-government (**1867**) Suez Canal opened (**1869**) Education Act (**1870**) Compulsory elementary schooling for all. Franco-Prussian War (**1870–1871**) First Anglo-Boer War (**1880**) Second Anglo-Boer War (**1899**)	
1900	Australia given self-government	**Saxe–Coburg–Gotha** Edward VII d. 1910

Contextualising ourselves

The texts we shall be looking at from the perspective of context reflect the social changes that took place over the 200 years summarised in the timeline. At the beginning of the eighteenth century ordinary people were no better educated than before, though there had been a bloodless revolution in 1688 which placed the Protestant William of Orange and his wife Mary, daughter of Charles II, on the throne, and Parliament's democratic powers were consolidated. Key thinkers of the period were the philosopher John Locke and the scientist Isaac Newton, with their emphasis on reason and the evidence of the senses. Society was stable and agrarian, though the beginnings of the industrial revolution emerged later in the century. However, poverty, corrupt local government and the severe penal laws made life hard for the poor. Britain continued to expand as a colonial power in India (East India Company), America and Canada, and (by 1788) in Australia. The loss of the American colonies, however, in 1776 was seen as a terrible blow. The French Revolution in 1789 profoundly affected the rest of Europe, and led to increasingly repressive regimes elsewhere.

At the beginning of the nineteenth century, we were at war with France; the industrial revolution was well underway, with people leaving the country to work in factories in the towns; employment conditions were harsh, child labour was exploited and the Poor Law desperately in need of reform; there was a terrible famine in Ireland; and the government was nervous and repressive. By the second half of the century social and educational reform was taking place, and the Victorian systems of water, sewage, transport which we still use today were being built (e.g. the London Underground, the railways network). The British Empire was at its height and British industry was at the forefront of the world. Wars continued to be fought across the world, and British troops were frequently involved in India, South Africa, the Crimea, or America – but there was relative peace at home.

There were radical changes in people's way of thinking about the world: the age of reason, with its emphasis on rational, scientific explanation and religious tolerance was being replaced by the age of revolution, which challenged the social and political *status quo* and urged new ways of thinking. For example, many Romantic writers rejected institutionalised religion in favour of more direct access to the divine through the world of Nature. By the mid-nineteenth century the novel had established itself as a powerful vehicle of social criticism in England. In America, writers were influenced by new ideas from Europe, but were still profoundly affected by the Puritan past. Women writers, following the traditions of the late seventeenth century, continued to be productive: dramatists and poets in particular flourished. By the late eighteenth century many women were writing fiction (e.g. the Gothic romances of Ann Radcliffe and the social comedies of Jane Austen), and in the nineteenth-century writers like the Brontë sisters (alias 'Currer, Ellis and Acton Bell'), Elizabeth Gaskell and 'George Eliot' (Marian Evans). Indeed, it was often thought that the main audience for literature (not just novels) was predominantly female and middle class!

ACTIVITY 40

The following list gives some idea of the extraordinary range of people and events prominent in this period. Choose an area/topic which interests you, and with a partner, investigate two or three people/events from the list. Present your joint findings to the group.

Royal Society *science*
Grub Street *journalism/publishing*
The Adam brothers *architecture and interior design*
William Hogarth *painting*
Spinning Jenny *industrial development*
Factory Acts *industrial welfare*

William Wilberforce *abolition of slavery*
Peterloo Massacre *political repression*
Battle of Waterloo *military campaign/ Napoleonic wars*
Reform Bill *political reform*
Great Exhibition *celebration of British achievement mid-century*
Indian Mutiny (Black Hole of Calcutta) *colonialism*
Pre-Raphaelites *art and design*
Isambard Brunel *technological development/civil engineering*

Part 1: Contextualising Poetry

The range of poetry produced in this period is immense and richly varied, not only in Britain, but also in America. If we were literary historians, we would be talking about the move from Classicism to Romanticism and beyond. But literary history is far from being our first aim. The extracts chosen do reveal something of the movements of literary history (any poet's work will reveal not only private feeling but also public experience), but the focus remains strictly on *contextualising* poetry within this complex period.

Developments in poetic form

Right through the eighteenth century, poets still preferred blank verse/ iambic pentameter (10 syllables /5 stressed) or tetrameter (8 syllables /4 stressed). There were experiments with the rhymed lyric (ode), but the sonnet remained popular. The rise of the ballad and hymn (at the end of the eighteenth century) reflects a new desire to include ordinary people, not just the educated establishment, as audiences for poetry. Indeed, in *Lyrical Ballads,* Wordsworth and Coleridge specifically aimed to use 'the language of men' rather than elaborate eighteenth-century poetic diction. There were new ways of using old forms. For example, Wordsworth's poem *Michael* has an old Lakeland shepherd as its 'epic hero' instead of the conventional prince or noble warrior; in a different kind of autobiographical epic (*The Prelude*), Wordsworth is his own 'hero', telling the story of the 'Growth of the Poet's Mind'. Later nineteenth-century poetic experiments include Tennyson's reworking of the traditional elegy or lament for the dead (*In Memoriam*), Robert Browning's dramatic monologues (*My Last Duchess, Fra Lippo Lippi*) and Gerard Manley Hopkins's 'sprung rhythm' – it is a rich period for poetry!

a Alexander Pope (1688–1744)

Frail in health (though not in mind or temperament), Pope was a
distinguished translator of Greek and Latin epic, a wit and satirist, and
intimate friend of many important literary, political and aristocratic figures
of the age.

From The Dunciad Book IV The Triumph of Dullness

Then blessing all, 'Go children of my care!
To practice now from theory repair.
All my commands are easy, short and full:
My sons! Be proud, be selfish, and be dull …'
More had she spoke, but yawned – All Nature nods:
What mortal can resist the Yawn of Gods?
Churches and chapels instantly it reached;
(St. James's first, for leaden Gilbert preached)
Then catched the schools; the Hall scarce kept awake;
The Convocation gaped, but could not speak:
Lost was the Nation's Sense, nor could be found,
While the long solemn unison went round:
Wide, and more wide, it spread o'er all the realm;
Even Palinurus nodded at the helm:
The vapour mild o'er each committee crept;
Unfinished treaties in each office slept;
And chiefless armies dozed out the campaign;
And navies yawned for orders on the main.

Dullness – the Goddess
Palinurus – the helmsman of Aeneas – here, the Prime Minister, Sir Robert Walpole
Gilbert – Dr John Gilbert, Dean of Exeter
Hall – Westminster Hall
Convocation – a clergy assembly which had not met since 1717
Unfinished treaties etc. – all examples of government incompetence

Context of text: this extract is taken from the end of Book Four of *The
Dunciad* (1743). Books One to Three were written some years earlier
(1728) as a comic mock-epic attack on Pope's critics, the despised literary
hacks and journalists (e.g. 'Grub Street'). As a distinguished translator of
Homer, Pope enjoyed parodying everything classical in his vitriolic attack
(one example being a spectacular mud fight). However, in Book Four,
Pope becomes more serious, and writes in a bitterly satiric tone about the
social, political and moral corruption of contemporary society, where the
Goddess Dullness rules, and one final yawn (described in the extract) will
bring about the Apocalypse. The *genre* is a mocking version of the Greek
and Roman epic poems about great heroes like Odysseus and Aeneas. The
verse form is the rhyming couplet (sometimes called the heroic couplet).

Context of production: Pope remarked that 'the life of a wit is warfare on
earth' and this aptly describes his position as satirist when he completed
The Dunciad. A brilliant classical scholar and translator, Pope had earlier in
his career written a light mock-epic (*The Rape of the Lock*), romantic nature
poetry (*Windsor Forest*), personal poems (*Epistle to Dr Arbuthnot*) as well as
moral philosophy (*Essay on Man*). His intention in *The Dunciad* (1743) is

to warn of the spiritual and moral dangers within his contemporary society, with everything from education to philosophy corrupted and destroyed:

Lo! thy dread Empire, CHAOS is restored:
Light dies before thy uncreating word:
Thy hand, great Anarch! Lets the curtain fall;
And Universal Darkness buries All.

He died the following year.

Context of reception: the audience for Pope's poetry was large, and included the political establishment of the day as well as distinguished literary and intellectual circles. His precocious early successes as a poet unfortunately meant that he made many enemies among less talented writers ('Grub Street') and was endlessly attacked in pamphlets, satiric verses and newspapers. This makes for a complex audience for this final version of *The Dunciad* (the 1728 version was an obvious attack on the commercialisation of the arts); those in sympathy with Pope would have admired its moral courage, whereas his enemies might have chosen to *read* it simply as an allegory (story with a moral) rather than an indictment of society as a whole. Hence the *reading position* would have been 'for or against Pope'. Today (**context of immediate situation**) this kind of poem is hard to read, and quickly discarded. Because modern readers know little about early eighteenth-century social and literary history (**context of cultural frame of reference**) this poem (and similar poems by the 'wits' of the period) seems impenetrable, and may even be judged as trivial and frivolous. (For example, a feminist reading might see this extract as representative of patriarchal power at its height, with all bases of power – church, government, armed services – entirely masculine).

ACTIVITY 41

In the passages below we can compare the comic strategies used by two satirists writing over 250 years apart. In the episode from *The Dunciad* cited previously Pope is using the comic idea of an enormous yawn spreading across society to make a serious point about the spread of moral and spiritual corruption. In Simon Hoggart's parliamentary diary column (*The Guardian* 13.12.01) the writer is also using humour for a serious purpose. Look for examples of different comic strategies (e.g. making folly look ridiculous, exaggeration, irony etc.) in *both texts*.

The House of Commons can be a cruel place, like the Roman Colosseum or a school playground.

And yesterday Labour MPs were in a cruel mood. They know that the NHS is in crisis, recession is on the way, and our public transport is like India's, only less reliable. But there is one consolation: however badly the government is doing, the Tories are doing worse. Every week Labour MPs gather for Prime Minister's question time to celebrate that and rub it in.

Poor Iain Duncan Smith hardly stands a chance. . . . He does make careful preparations. At 3pm, to combat the frog in his throat, Mr Duncan Smith pops a soothing sweetie in his mouth. As his moment approaches, the sweetie hurls around his mouth, up and down, left to right, back and forth, like a pair of Y-fronts in a tumble dryer.

It doesn't help much. He still seems about to choke on the third word of every sentence, as if he were suffering from some grief so intense and so profound that none of us have ever experienced it. How he will sound if something really sad happens I do not know . . .

To make things worse, he has decided the way to become charismatic is to shout out random words. Or just last words. Talking about the Blair plans for health spending, he suddenly yelled out: 'Eight percent is vacuous!' and Labour MPs went 'Ooooh!' in mock terror.

Later he said the £1m payment for the new chief executive of Railtrack was 'absolutely ridiculous!' and they all went 'Whoooo!', like parents pretending to be scared on the dodgems.

When Tony Blair blamed the state of the railways on the botched privatisation, IDS said: 'There he goes again!' which worked fine for Ronald Reagan in his debate with Jimmy Carter, but sounded petty yesterday. When he finally sat down to loud Labour cheers, John Prescott shouted: 'Get up again!'

b Christina Rossetti (1830–1893)

Although Rossetti was closely connected with the literary and artistic world of the Pre-Raphaelites via her brother, she was nevertheless a successful poet in her own right. An early broken engagement (she found her fiancé's Roman Catholicism unacceptable to her high Anglicanism) may be reflected in her poems about unhappy or frustrated love.

Amor Mundi

'Oh where are you going with your love-locks flowing,
  On the west wind blowing along this valley track?
'The downhill path is easy, come with me an it please ye,
  We shall escape the uphill by never turning back.'

So they two went together in glowing August weather,
  The honey-breathing heather lay to their left and right;
And dear she was to dote on, her swift feet seemed to float on
  The air like soft twin pigeons too sportive to alight.

'Oh, what is that in heaven where grey cloud-flakes are seven,
  Where blackest clouds hang riven just at the rainy skirt?'
'Oh, that's a meteor sent us, the message dumb, portentous, –
  An undeciphered solemn signal of help or hurt.'

'Oh, what is that glides quickly where velvet flowers grow thickly,
  Their scent comes rich and sickly?' – 'A scaled and hooded worm.'
'Oh, what's that in the hollow, so pale I quake to follow?'
  Oh, that's a thin dead body which waits the eternal term.'

'Turn again, O my sweetest, – turn again, false and fleetest:
  This way whereof thou weetest I fear is hell's own track.'
'Nay, too steep for hill-mounting; nay, too late for cost-counting:
  This downhill path is easy, but there's no turning back.'

Glossary: *Amor Mundi* – love of the world (Latin)

The first thing to strike most modern readers (**context of text** and **context of immediate situation**) is probably the odd language scattered through the poem ('an it please ye', 'riven', 'worm', 'whereof', 'weetest'). The *ballad* form adopted by Rossetti is relatively familiar, though she does use the less common hexameter (12 syllable) line. However, the rest of the poem is in the straight ballad tradition, using alternate rhyme and the question/answer format to tell the story. However, there are still some difficulties with the language; not only does Rossetti use archaic vocabulary but also archaic syntax ('whereof thou weetest').

The reason for this is directly linked with two other contexts: the **context of production** and the **context of cultural reference**. Through her brother Dante Gabriel Rossetti, a founding member of the Pre-Raphaelite Brotherhood (1848), Christina Rossetti was familiar with their interest in the mediaeval world. A group of artists and writers (e.g. Millais, Holman Hunt, Burne-Jones), the Pre-Raphaelites were drawn to fourteenth-century Italian painting, and its clear and bright representations of the natural world. Their nostalgia for mediaeval times was combined with a strong dislike of Victorian ugliness, and a sense of moral purpose. William Morris, architect, poet and social reformer also joined the group and became one of its most famous members. Hence Christina Rossetti's use of the ballad form and some archaic vocabulary.

What is the poem about (**context of text**)? It seems to centre on a mistaken decision: the two participants in the dialogue (probably male and female) are walking through a valley in deep summer, and one persuades the other to take the downhill track (the landscape may be symbolic). Rossetti tells the story from alternate perspectives. The *reader* (**context of immediate situation**) picks up – through the descriptions of nature – clues that something sinister is happening, and the chilling conclusion in the final line is 'there's no turning back'. Although we have no information about the **context of reception** of this particular poem, we know that Rossetti's extensive publications were well received. More recent critics have been keen to apply feminist and Freudian readings to her poems about innocence corrupted, as in *Goblin Market* (1862).

ACTIVITY 42

Look at *Amor Mundi* and the unseen poem below (both written by women in the mid-nineteenth century) and answer the following questions:

a What evidence can you find in the poems of the context of cultural reference? Give examples for each.

b Both poems are based upon a kind of symbolic journey. How effectively do you think each poet uses this idea within her poem? Which poem do you find more successful? Find examples to support your judgment. You may like to work with a partner on this.

Unseen poem

Because I could not stop for Death –
He kindly stopped for me –
The Carriage held but just Ourselves –
And Immortality.

We slowly drove – He knew no haste
And I had put away

My labor and my leisure too,
For His Civility –

We passed the School, where Children strove
At Recess – in the Ring –
We passed the Fields of Gazing Grain –
We passed the Setting Sun –

Or rather – He passed Us –
The Dews drew quivering and chill –
For only Gossamer, my Gown –
My Tippet – only Tulle –

We paused before a House that seemed
A Swelling of the Ground –
The Roof was scarcely visible –
The Cornice – in the Ground –

Since then – 'tis Centuries – and yet
Feels shorter than the Day
I first surmised the Horses Heads
Were toward Eternity –

Part 2: Contextualising Literary Prose

This is the great period of the novel in English: just look at the following list:

Eighteenth century
Henry Fielding (*Tom Jones*)
Samuel Richardson (*Pamela*)
Lawrence Sterne (*Tristram Shandy*)
Ann Radcliffe (*Mysteries of Udolpho*)
James Fenimore Cooper (*Last of the Mohicans*)

Nineteenth century
Jane Austen (*Mansfield Park*)
Charlotte Brontë (*Jane Eyre*)
Emily Brontë (*Wuthering Heights*)
Anne Brontë (*The Tenant of Wildfell Hall*)
Elizabeth Gaskell (*North and South*)
Charles Dickens (*David Copperfield*)
W.M. Thackeray (*Vanity Fair*)
Nathaniel Hawthorne (*The Scarlet Letter*)
Herman Melville (*Moby Dick*)
George Eliot (*The Mill on the Floss*)
Thomas Hardy (*The Mayor of Casterbridge*).

What do lists like this tell us? They are only representative (one title per author), but they do give us a *cumulative* sense that in this period the novel was the runaway genre of the period (despite strong competition from poetry). The novel seemed to fulfil the needs of writers keen to depict dramatic social and political change, to show the real world of poverty as well as riches, and to appeal to a public increasingly interested in written narrative. Moreover, new methods of publication (e.g. serial/magazine/periodical) made it possible for the reading audience to include working class as well as traditional middle and upper class readers.

It's worth noting some characteristic features of the novel at this period, which include the use of the authorial voice (often ironic or humorous), realistic characterisation and descriptions of place, careful representation of feeling or sensibility, and a clear sense of social hierarchy.

a Elizabeth Gaskell (1810–1865)

Born in rural Cheshire, Gaskell married a Unitarian minister whose pastoral duties included caring for the urban poor. Her first novel, *Mary Barton* was written to distract herself after the death of her first child. She was highly regarded by many distinguished people in Victorian society, for her humanitarian work, her beauty and her appealing personality. She was also the first biographer of Charlotte Brontë.

From Mary Barton (1848)

Barton growled inarticulate words of no benevolent import to a large class of mankind [the rich manufacturers], and so they went along till they arrived in Berry Street. It was unpaved; and down the middle a gutter forced its way, every now and then forming pools in the holes with which the street abounded. Never was the Old Edinburgh cry of 'Gardez l'eau' [emptying of chamber pots] more necessary than in this street. As they passed, women from their doors tossed household slops of *every* description into the gutter; they ran into the next pool, which overflowed and stagnated. Heaps of ashes were the stepping-stones, on which the passer-by, who cared in the least for cleanliness, took care not to put his foot. Our friends were not dainty, but even they picked their way till they got to some steps leading down into a small area, where a person standing would have his head about one foot below the level of the street, and might at the same time, without the least motion of his body, touch the window of the cellar and the damp muddy wall right opposite. You went down one step even from the foul area into the cellar in which a family of human beings lived. It was very dark inside. The window panes were many of them broken and stuffed with rags, which was reason enough for the dusky light that pervaded the place even at mid-day. After the account I have given of the state of the street, no-one can be surprised that on going into the cellar inhabited by Davenport [the sick worker], the smell was so foetid as almost to knock the two men down. Quickly recovering themselves, as those inured to such things do, they began to penetrate the thick darkness of the place, and to see three or four little children rolling on the damp, nay wet, brick floor, through which the stagnant, filthy moisture of the street oozed up; the fire-place was empty and black; the wife sat on her husband's chair, and cried in the dank loneliness.
'See, missis, I'm back again. – Hold your noise, children, and don't mither your mammy for bread, here's a chap as has got some for you.'
   In that dim light, which was darkness to strangers, they clustered round Barton, and tore from him the food that he had brought with him. It was a large hunch of bread, but it had vanished in an instant.

Elizabeth Gaskell wrote as an accurate observer of the squalor of Manchester slums (**context of production** and **context of cultural reference**). Her account of the appalling conditions for factory workers in the 'hungry forties' is confirmed by what Friedrich Engels reported in his *Condition of the Working Class in England* (1845).(Karl Marx would later make use of Engels's findings in *Das Kapital* (1867)). Gaskell makes the point in *Mary Barton* that the relationship between employers and workers is bad because neither has any real understanding of the other. Naturally the poor suffered most from this mutual ignorance. Although there is no mention of Mary Barton herself in this extract, it is nevertheless a key episode in the novel (**context of text**). The horror in the cellar, and its tragic outcome, make John Barton resolve to stand up for the poor as an early trades unionist. Gaskell tells a good story too – this is not simply a story with a moral message (i.e. a didactic novel). There is romance (Mary is torn between two potential lovers: an employer's son and a mill engineer) and drama (a murder, and a last minute dash for a witness to clear her accused lover's name). Interspersed with the narrative are many vivid scenes of industrial life, and many tragic and unnecessary deaths from starvation, disease and accident. It is a grim book in many ways, but it is important in the history of the novel. No book before had focused so completely on working-class characters.

Perhaps unsurprisingly, the novel was received with great hostility by Manchester mill-owners and the Tory press (**context of reception**); however, it was much admired by writers like Charles Dickens, who also attacked the exploitation of the poor in *Bleak House* (1852–3) and industrialisation in *Hard Times* (1854). Today we read the novel (**context of immediate situation**) as a terrible indictment of the *past*, often forgetting that comparable poverty still exists. A *historicist* reading would focus on the way Gaskell reproduces the actual conditions of the industrial poor; a *feminist* reading might note the way in which patriarchal power is exercised to confirm, rather than challenge, gender positions. Whether Gaskell, writing as a woman, takes a different stance from a male writer with similar first-hand experience is impossible to tell. It is clear, however, that Gaskell knew very well what she was doing when she wrote so graphically about the intimate relationship between industrialism and human suffering.

ACTIVITY 43

Compare Gaskell's description of poverty and suffering on page 85 with the first-hand account below. It is taken from a remarkable collection of testimonies recorded by Henry Mayhew and published in the *Morning Chronicle* between 19 October 1849 and 12 December 1850. They were later to form the basis of Mayhew's book *London Labour and the London Poor* (1851 and 1861).

'Between ten and eleven years ago I was left a widow with two young children, and far advanced in pregnancy with another. I had no means of getting a living, and therefore I thought I would take up slop-work. [*clothes manufacturing*] I got work at slop-shirts – what they call second-hand. I had no security, and therefore could not get the work myself from the warehouse. Two months before I was confined, I seemed to do middling well. I could manage three or four shirts – at 3d. each, by sitting closely at work from five or six in the morning till about nine or ten at night; but of course when I was confined I was unable to do anything. As soon as I was able to sit up I undertook slop-shirts again; but my child being sickly, I was not able to earn as much as before. Perhaps I could earn 9d. a day by hard work, when I get 3d. each shirt; but sometimes I only get 2½d. And I have been obliged to do them at 1½d. each, and with my child sickly, could only earn 4d., or at most 6d. a day. . . . 1s. 9d. a week went for rent; and as to a living, I don't call it that; I was so reduced with it, and my child being so bad, it couldn't be considered a living. I was obliged to live on potatoes and salt; and for nine weeks together I lived on potatoes, and never knew what it was to have a half-quartern loaf . . . my health was declining, And I wasn't able to do hard work. My child's health, too, was declining, and I was obliged to pawn the sheets of my bed and my blankets to procure a shilling . . . I became so reduced . . . that I was obliged to get an order to get into the 'house'. [*workhouse*] I didn't wish to go in, but I wanted relief and knew I couldn't get it without doing so. I felt it a hard trial to have my children taken from my bosom . . . they little thought that we were so soon to be parted. The first was seven years old, the second three, and the infant was in my arms. A mother's feelings are better felt than described. The children were taken and separated and then, oh my God! what I felt no tongue can tell.' [*shortly after all three children died*]

b Mark Twain (1835–1910)

His real name was Samuel Langhorne Clemens, but he took this pen-name from the riverboatmen's cry on the Mississippi as they measured the river depth off shore. He was a successful newspaperman and humorist, whose best-known novels recreate his own childhood in Hannibal, Missouri.

From The Adventures of Huckleberry Finn (1885)

We went drifting down into a big bend, and the night clouded up and got hot. The river was very wide, and was walled with solid timber on both sides; you couldn't see a break in it hardly ever, or a light. We talked about Cairo, and wondered whether we would know it when we got to it. I said likely we wouldn't, because I had heard say there warn't but about a dozen houses there, and if they didn't happen to have them lit up, how was we going to know we was passing a town? Jim said if the two big rivers [Mississippi and Ohio] joined together there, that would show. But I said maybe we might think we was passing the foot of an island and coming into the same old river again. That disturbed Jim – and me too . . .

There warn't nothing to do, now, but to look out sharp for the town, and not pass it without seeing it. He said he'd be mighty sure to see it, because he'd be a free man the minute he seen it, but if he missed it he'd be in the slave country again and no more show for freedom. Every little while he jumps up and says:
   'Dah she is!'
But it warn't. It was Jack-o-lanterns, or lightning bugs; so he set down again, and went to watching, same as before. Jim said it made him all over trembly and feverish to be so close to freedom. Well, I can tell you it made me all over trembly and feverish, too, to hear him, because I begun to get it through my head that he *was* most free – and who was to blame for it? Why, *me*. I couldn't get that out of my conscience, no how nor no way. It got to troubling me so I couldn't rest; I couldn't stay still in one place. It hadn't ever come home to me before, what this thing was that I was doing. But now it did; and it staid with me, and scorched me more and more.

The **context of text** places this novel in the *picaresque* genre: Huck Finn, the son of the local drunk, has run away to avoid the awful effects of 'sivilisation', in company with a runaway slave. They drift down the Mississippi on a raft, stopping off at various river-towns and villages, providing Twain with the opportunity for much sharp social criticism as well as humour. The fact that the entire narrative is in the voice of Huck (first person) is important, partly because of the perspective offered by an innocent eye on the adult world, and partly because of Huck's language: Twain is very careful to describe the exact dialect used. He and Jim (and others) speak non-standard American English in a variety of dialects, but it is not to be assumed that they are either inarticulate or uneducated in the broadest sense. The **context of cultural reference** obviously includes the whole world of the river, its customs and practices, as well as the central issue of slavery. In this passage Huck is divided between what one critic has called his 'sound heart' and 'deformed conscience'. In terms of the **context of production**, Twain's experience as a riverboat pilot on the Mississippi, as well as his own pre-Civil War childhood in Hannibal, Missouri, gave him ample preparation. Written in two parts, the first (1876) ending just after this extract, and the second resumed in 1879, Twain revisited the Mississippi valley of his childhood and wrote it up in *Life on the Mississippi* (1883). Reinvigorated, he then completed *Huckleberry Finn* (1884–5). The novel was published as a sequel to *The Adventures of Tom Sawyer* (1876), and although very different from the earlier boys' adventure story, was well received. It has never gone out of print since (**context of reception**).

In the **context of immediate situation**, the novel can be read differently by different age groups, as an adventure story or as a profoundly moral critique of American society. Admired by writers as varied as Henry James, T.S. Eliot and Ernest Hemingway, *The Adventures of Huckleberry Finn* retains its universal appeal. *Historicist, Marxist* and *Freudian* interpretations can all be made.

ACTIVITY 44

Both Elizabeth Gaskell and Mark Twain have important criticisms to make about their own society in the extracts above.

a Identify the targets of their criticism.

b Compare the literary strategies each adopts to make his or her point.

c What effect do you think each extract has on a modern reader?

Unseen literary prose

The old men on the rising straw-rick talked of the past days when they had been accustomed to thresh with flails on the oaken barn-floor; when everything, even to winnowing, was effected by hand labour, which to their thinking, though slow, produced better results. Those, too, on the corn-rick talked a little; but the perspiring ones at the [threshing] machine, including Tess, could not lighten their duties by the exchange of many words. It was the ceaselessness of the work which tried her so severely, and began to make her wish that she had never come to Flintcomb-Ash. The women on the corn-rick – Marian, who was one of them, in particular, – could stop to drink ale or cold tea from the flagon now and then, or to exchange a few gossiping remarks while they wiped their faces or cleared the fragments of straw or husk from their clothing; but for Tess there was no respite; for as the drum never stopped, the man who fed it could not stop, and she, who had to supply the man with untied sheaves, could not stop either, unless Marian changed places with her, which she sometimes did for half an hour in spite of [Farmer] Groby's objection that she was too slow-handed for a feeder.

ACTIVITY 45

The writer of the above extract (male, late nineteenth century) presents the women workers as victims of the machine age in farming. To what extent could this text be read from the feminist position, as an example of patriarchy disempowering women? What textual evidence can you find to support this reading?

Part 3: Contextualising Drama

After the flowering of Restoration theatre, drama continued to flourish in the eighteenth century; plays like Farquar's *The Recruiting Officer* (1706) and Susannah Centlivre's *The Gamester* (1705) were popular, together with more sentimental plays like Cibber's *The Careless Husband* (1704). Centlivre's *The Wonder: A Woman Keeps a Secret* (1714) later gave David Garrick one of his most successful parts. This remarkable actor dominated the theatre between 1740 and 1776. Richard Sheridan (*The School for Scandal* 1777) and Oliver Goldsmith (*She Stoops to Conquer* 1773) played at the major theatres at Covent Garden and Drury Lane. The theatre was also increasingly popular in America – the first American comedy was *The Contrast* (1787) by Royall Tyler. In the nineteenth century, melodrama replaced the lighter comedy of Sheridan et al. It was the time of great actor-managers and actresses – these included Edmund and Charles Kean, John Philip Kemble, Mrs Siddons, Henry Irving and Ellen Terry (a great-great-aunt of John Gielgud). By the end of the century, dramatists like Oscar Wilde (*The Importance of Being Earnest*) and Arthur Pinero (*The Second Mrs Tanqueray*) flourished. Their plays tended to reflect a quieter, more natural style of acting.

a Richard Sheridan (1751–1816)

Sheridan's own life was romantic rather like his plays, in that he fell in love and eloped with a young singer against both families' wishes. They married, and he wrote *The Rivals* to earn some desperately needed money. It was a great success, and his career as a playwright was established. Eventually he went into Parliament and became a politician, though financial instability continued to dog him.

From The Rivals (1775) Act 3 Scene 3

Mrs Malaprop and *Captain Absolute* in *Mrs Malaprop's Lodgings*

Mrs Mal. Your being Sir Anthony's son, captain, would be itself a sufficient accommodation; but from the ingenuity of your appearance, I am convinced you deserve the character here given you.

Abs. Permit me to say, madam, that as I never yet have had the pleasure of seeing Miss Languish, my principal inducement in this affair at present is the honour of being allied to Mrs Malaprop; of whose intellectual accomplishments, elegant manners, and unaffected learning, no tongue is silent.

Mrs Mal. Sir, you do me infinite honour! I beg, captain, you'll be seated. – Ah! few gentlemen, now-a-days, know how to value the ineffectual qualities in a woman! – few think how a little knowledge becomes a gentlewoman. – Men have no sense now but for the worthless flower of beauty!

Abs. It is but too true, indeed, ma'am; – yet I fear our ladies should share the blame – they think our admiration of beauty so great, that knowledge in them would be superfluous. Thus, like garden-trees, they seldom show fruit, till time has robbed them of more specious blossom. – few, like Mrs Malaprop and the orange-tree, are rich in both at once!

Mrs Mal. Sir, you overpower me with good breeding. – he is the very pine-apple of politeness! – you are not ignorant, captain, that this giddy girl has somehow contrived to fix her affections on a beggarly, strolling, eavesdropping ensign, whom none of us have seen, and nobody knows anything of.

Abs. Oh, I have heard the silly affair before.– I'm not at all prejudiced against her on that account.

Mrs Mal. You are very good and very considerate, captain. I am sure I have done everything in my power since I exploded the affair ... But I am sorry to say, she seems resolved to decline every particle I enjoin her.

Abs. It must be very distressing, indeed, ma'am.

Mrs Mal. Oh! It gives me the hydrostatics to such a degree. – ... this very day, I have interceded another letter from the fellow; I believe I have it in my pocket.

Abs. Oh, the devil! my last note. [*Aside*]

The Rivals (**context of production**), written when Sheridan was only twenty three, was a great success (**context of reception**). It reflected some personal experience and also something of Bath society, where his father Thomas, an actor-manager, and his mother, Frances, a well-known novelist, were prominent. Following in the tradition of Restoration comedy (**context of text**), the tone of *The Rivals* is less biting and satirical. In the extract the hero, Captain Absolute, is inwardly laughing at his tricking of Mrs Malaprop, guardian of his beloved Lydia Languish, whom he has wooed in the guise of ' Ensign Beverley', a penniless young officer, rather than as himself, a rich heir to a baronetcy. The scene shows the absurdity of Mrs Malaprop's affected language and of the fact that she is urging a match between two people who are already secret lovers. The *comedy of manners* genre usually includes a love plot, a sub-plot, and a mixture of high and low life (i.e. usually upper-class and servant-class). Mrs Malaprop is an unusual figure in that her role is not simply to be the dragon-guardian of the heroine, but to interest and amuse the audience in her own right.

The play gains in significance when the socio-economic background is explored (**context of cultural reference**). The position of women in contemporary upper-class or upper middle-class society is clear; marriage on the basis of money, rank and status is the appropriate outcome (and for young men too). The role of parents or guardians is to ensure this, regardless of inclination or 'love'. In *The Rivals* nothing can really go wrong because we know from the beginning that Absolute and Lydia love each other *and* are socially suitable. The interest is in the intrigue, and in Mrs Malaprop, who in her absurd way represents important current concerns about female education. The issue across Europe was to what degree were women capable of rationality! In England a tradition of educated women had already been established by women like Margaret Cavendish and Mary Astell, as well as by female dramatists, poets and novelists. At the time Sheridan was writing, however, such open attitudes to female education were again under threat.

ACTIVITY 46

Modern *readers* may find this text a little difficult (modern *audiences* on the other hand have few problems, once they 'get into' the language, which doesn't usually take more than a few minutes). Working with a partner, answer the following questions:

a Identify and correct Mrs Malaprop's errors.
b Try rewriting this extract in modern English, noting which parts of the dialogue were particularly difficult to 'translate'.

b Victorian melodrama

Melodramas were written for popular theatres in London between 1780–1850, combining sensational and romantic drama (often violent) with music. Their appeal was to a relatively unsophisticated audience, but they were extremely successful.

From Maria Marten or the Murder in the Red Barn

Act 1 Scene 1 (1840) A festive occasion. Villagers discovered dancing . . . on the Green. *Maria Marten* leading the dance . . . Villain's music heard in distance. *William Corder* enters at back. He looks round and leers at *Maria.* Villain's music grows louder.

Corder [tapping leggings with riding whip in a sinister way]: Egad, that's the pretty girl who has occupied my thoughts so much since I've been here.

Marten: Why it's Mister Corder! I'm glad to see you here, Sir, to honour our homely festivities. I heard you had arrived in our village some days ago. Will you join our merrymaking?

Corder: Thanks for your kind welcome. Who is that charming girl?

Marten: Why, have you forgotten her? It's my daughter Maria [beckons her; *Maria* skips towards him. Soft music] This is William Corder, son of our landlord.

Corder: Miss Marten may I claim your hand for the next dance?

Maria [curtly]: Excuse me, Sir, but I never dance with strangers. [trips away, nose in the air]

... *Corder* (alone). Villain's music; stage slowly darkens.

Corder: Pretty and coy, yet she shall be mine for I feel I love and have set my heart on possessing her. She seems to shrink from my advances. I must overcome her scruples. How? Tomorrow is Polestead Fair, all the lads and lasses will assemble in the village, there must I gain an introduction to her [Music very loud; shouting above it.]

And all the arts that flattery can devise

I'll use to make her mine [crashing chord. Slinks away.]

Act 1 Scene 3 Polestead village green. A Booth on each side of the stage. ... Faint strains of the Villain's music.

Maria: Ah, the gentleman coming asked me to dance with him, the very one the Gipsy spoke of. How my heart beats! I feel I want to fly...his presence...yet something keeps me on this spot. [*William Corder* strides on]

Corder: She is there again and if the Gipsy has fulfilled his part, matters stand easy for my wooing! Miss Marten, I am glad to see you at the Fair, but I see you have no one to escort you round. Will you accept my humble services?

Maria: Oh Sir, what will people say to see Maria Marten the poor labourer's daughter in company with the son of the rich Mr Corder?

Corder: Why, that William Corder has too much manhood to see a poor girl go unprotected in a scene of wild confusion. Come, shall I take you in these shows?

Maria: No, thank you, Mister Corder, I have no wish for such sights, but if you will aid me to find my sister I shall be thankful ...

Corder: ... allow me to see you safely home.

Maria: I thank you, the road is somewhat lonely and –

Corder: And among these drunken labourers and gipsy vagrants you will find a protector – nay no refusal. I'll see you safely to your own door [aside] and SO IS MY FIRST STEP GAINED. [Chord. Thunder.]

Melodramas like *Maria Marten* were enormously popular (**context of reception**). They were written rather sketchily to a formula, using improvisation (**context of production**), but appealed to local audiences with different special effects (real boats on stage at Sadler's Wells; horses at Hoxton; performing elephants in the City of London etc.).
Stock characters and situations also reflected changes in social attitudes e.g. to seduction (**context of cultural reference**). In the eighteenth century heroines threatened with seduction tended to survive unscathed. In Victorian melodrama (influenced by Romantic ideas about the value of the individual), whatever happened to a heroine her purity of soul was secure. *Maria Marten* was based on an actual crime; the real William Corder murdered his former lover, Maria Marten on 18 May 1827, and buried the body in the Red Barn, where it was exhumed the following year. Corder was hanged on 18 August 1828 in front of 10,000 people in Bury St. Edmunds.

a Write a scene from a Victorian melodrama using as many of stereotypical features listed below as possible. You may like to do this in pairs or as individuals. Suggest reasons for the popularity of melodrama.

- villain usually gentleman
- heroine usually innocent (often from country) and noble
- stereotypical costume (cloak, riding whip with villain)
- characteristic music associated with hero/heroine/villain
- dramatic event (seduction, murder)
- elderly well-meaning parents
- mysterious alien figure (Gipsy, Jew)
- sub-plot with low comedy.

b What aspects of the dramatist's contemporary society (*context of cultural reference*) are being criticised in this extract? What textual evidence can be found in this extract to support the idea that comedy is a strategy for criticising society?

Part 4: Contextualising Non-Literary Prose

The range of non-literary prose in English during this period is enormous, reflecting the complexity of eighteenth- and nineteenth-century society in Britain, America and the other colonies. Politics, philosophy, literary theory, religion, aesthetic theory, history, journals and letters, books of education, public reports, scientific writing – the possibilities were endless and the practitioners numerous. As literacy increased, and the desire for self-improvement took root within the working class, people's thirst for learning, for knowledge and information was enormous. The extracts chosen below reflect both public and private experience.

a James Boswell (1740–1795)

Trained as a lawyer, Boswell was much more interested in literature and politics, and was something of a celebrity hunter in this world. He first met Dr Samuel Johnson in 1763, and became an admirer and friend of the distinguished scholar, poet and lexicographer.

From The Journal of a Tour to the Hebrides with Samuel Johnson LL.D (1773)

Joseph reported that the wind was still against us. Dr Johnson said, 'A wind, or not a wind? that is the question'; for he can amuse himself at times with a little play of words, or rather, sentences ... I must again and again apologise to fastidious readers, for recalling such minute particulars. They prove the scrupulous fidelity of my *Journal*. Dr Johnson said it was a very exact picture of a portion of his life.

While we were chatting in the indolent stile of men who were to stay here all this day at least, we were suddenly roused at being told that the wind was fair ... and that Mr Simpson's vessel was about to sail. Hugh M'Donald, the skipper, came to us, and was impatient that we should get ready, which we soon did. Dr. Johnson, with composure and solemnity, repeated the observation of Epictetus, that, 'as man has the voyage of death before him, whatever may be his employment, he should be ready at the master's call; and an old man should never be far from the shore, lest he should not be able to get himself ready'. He rode, and I and the other gentlemen walked, about an English mile to the shore, where the vessel lay. Dr Johnson said he should never forget Sky, and returned thanks for all civilities. We were carried to the vessel in a small boat which she had, and we set sail very briskly about one o'clock. Dr Johnson grew sick, and retired under cover, as it rained a good deal. I kept above, that I might have fresh air, and finding myself not affected by the motion of the vessel, I exulted in being a stout seaman, while Dr Johnson was quite in a state of annihilation. But I was soon humbled; for after imagining that I could go with ease to America or the East Indies, I became very sick, but kept above board, though it rained hard.

When Dr Johnson and James Boswell took this trip in the late summer and early autumn of 1773, the former was sixty, the latter only in his early thirties (**context of production**), and heir to Lord Auchinleck (pronounced 'Affleck'). Boswell's *Journal of a Tour of the Hebrides* appeared the year after Johnson's death in 1785, and his famous biography, *The Life of Samuel Johnson*, in 1791. The journal was evidently intended for publication, and gives us a strong sense of Boswell's personality as well as Dr Johnson's (**context of text**). As a Lowlands Scot, Boswell was interested in Johnson's English perspective on life in the Highlands. At this period large numbers of Scots were emigrating to the New World because of the Highland Clearances, with sheep replacing people on the great estates (**context of cultural reference**). This extract relates a simple incident with some wry self-mockery, conveys respectful admiration of Johnson's scholarly good humour, and presents a vivid picture of the discomforts of Hebridean sea passages. In the **context of reception**, this *Journal of a Tour to the Hebrides* has continued to be warmly received since its first publication. Boswell's reputation rests almost entirely on his work as Johnson's biographer and friend. Modern readers unfamiliar with the literary and political history of the eighteenth century are, however, likely to find both *Journal* and *Life* difficult in terms of local reference. More importantly, through Boswell's skills, the personality, values and wit of Johnson can be readily recognised and enjoyed.

b William Bartram (1739–1823)

William Bartram was a Quaker botanist from Philadelphia, Pennsylvania, who travelled widely in the southern United States, and recorded his travels and scientific discoveries.

From Travels through North and South Carolina, Georgia, East and West Florida . . . (1791)

The evening was temperately cool and calm. The crocodiles began to roar and appear in uncommon numbers along the shores and in the river. I fixed my camp in the open plain, near the utmost projection of the promontory, under the shelter of a large Live Oak, which stood on the highest part of the ground, and but a few yards from my boat.

From this open, high situation, I had a free prospect of the river, which was a matter of no trivial consideration to me, having good reason to dread the subtle attacks of the alligators, who were crowding about my harbour. . . . I determined to take my bob and try for some trout. About one hundred yards above my harbour began a cove or bay of the river, out of which opened a large lagoon. . . . its entrance and shores within I observed to be verged with floating lawns of the Pistia and Nymphea and other aquatic plants; these I knew were excellent haunts for trout … as the sun was near setting, and the alligators gathered around my harbour from all quarters; … I concluded to be expeditious in my trip to the lagoon [and] furnished myself with a club for my defence … and penetrating the first line of those which surrounded my harbour, they gave way; but being pursued by several very large ones, I … paddled with all my might towards the entrance to the lagoon … but ere I had half-way reached the place, I was attacked on all sides, several endeavouring to overset the canoe. My situation now became precarious to the last degree: two very large ones attacked me closely, at the same instant, rushing up with their heads and part of their bodies above the water, roaring terribly and belching floods of water over me. They struck their jaws together so close to my ears, as almost to stun me, and I expected every moment to be dragged out of the boat and instantly devoured, but I applied my weapons so effectually about me, though at random, that I was so successful as to beat them off a little; when, finding that they designed to renew the battle, I made for the shore … saving myself, by jumping out of the canoe on shore, as it is easy to outwalk them on land, although comparatively as swift as lightning in the water.

Bartram's *Travels* (1791) was not only successful in America, but also widely read in Europe. Wordsworth and Coleridge both read the *Travels*, as did the French Romantic writer Chateaubriand. Coleridge made use of Bartram's landscapes in 'Kubla Khan' (**contexts of production and reception**). Bartram undertook these expeditions sometimes accompanied by native American guides, sometimes on his own. His task as traveller and scientist was to give precise information about location, plant and animal life; he also provided anthropological information about the native American tribes he visited. Despite the informational nature of the *genre* (**context of text**), the liveliness of Bartram's style, and his acute eye for the telling detail make his travel writing appealing to a range of audiences. Within the **context of cultural reference**, Bartram is typical of the Enlightenment world, with its focus on observation and experience as a basis for judgement. Moreover, his Quaker background made him unusually tolerant and accepting of the customs and conduct of the native Americans he encountered. Earlier in this passage, he mentions that his 'Indian companion' requested to be set on shore, and remarks, 'I readily complied with his desire, knowing the impossibility of compelling an Indian against his own inclinations'.

ACTIVITY 48

Boswell and Bartram both write about the experience of travelling more than two hundred years ago.

a What differences and similarities do you see between these two early examples of travel writing?

b Look at an example of travel writing from the twentieth/twenty-first century (try Jan Morris or Colin Thubron or a Sunday travel supplement) and note the differences and similarities between the eighteenth-century texts and modern travel writing.

Summary

In this chapter we have looked at a wide range of extracts within each broad genre, applied the **contexts model** as before, and endeavoured to show the flexibility as well as the intellectual rigour this approach can bring to our understanding of the complex and varied texts of this extraordinary period.

6 Context of Texts: The Modern Period

TIMELINE

Date	Event	Dynasty/Monarch
1900	Abbey Theatre Dublin founded (**1904**)	**Saxe-Coburg-Gotha**
	1st World War starts (**1914–1918**)	Edward VII d. 1910
	Easter Rising (**1916**) Russian Revolution (**1917**)	**Windsor**
	Establishment of Irish Free State (Republic of	George V d. 1936
	Eire) (**1920**)	
	General Strike (**1926**) Depression (**1929–35**)	
	Commonwealth created (**1931**)	Edward VIII abdicated 1936
	2nd World War (**1939–45**)	George VI d. 1952
	Battle of Britain (**1940**) Fall of France	
	USA and Soviet Union enter war (**1941**)	
	Partition of India and Pakistan (**1947**)	Elizabeth II
1950	NATO founded (**1949**)	
	Korean War Conquest of Everest (**1953**)	
	Suez Crisis (**1956**)	
	Berlin Wall built (**1961**)	
	President John Kennedy assassinated (**1963**)	
	Malcolm X assassinated (**1965**) Six Days War	
	(**1967**) Martin Luther King assassinated (**1968**)	
	Manned moon landing (**1968**)	
	Cold War begins (**1970**) American troops	
	withdraw from Vietnam (**1973**)	
	Falklands Campaign (**1982**)	
	End of Cold War	
	Reunification of East & West Germany (**1990**)	
	Iraq invades Kuwait – Gulf War (**1990**)	
2000	Destruction of World Trade Centre, New York (**11 Sept 2001**)	

Contextualising ourselves

In theory we shouldn't have anything like the problems contextualising ourselves in this relatively short period of a single century as we had in earlier chapters. Events are relatively recent, and *almost* within living memory (though every year fewer people are left who experienced the First World War). If one century spans approximately five generations, A Level Literature students reading this book now are the fifth generation of the twentieth century. Your grandparents may have first-hand experience of the Second World War, *their* grandparents might recall the trauma of the First World War. But beyond this, nothing. The blanks are filled in by history books, by representations in art, literature, film, music, documentaries, comedy (e.g. *Blackadder 1914–18* and *Dad's Army*), and by public events and traditions (e.g. music from the Last Night at the Proms and the poppies of Remembrance Day). Again, the timeline helps us out in reminding us of events over the past century which are ineradicable from our collective memory – revolutions in Russia and China, the death of colonialism, wars in the Far East, in the Middle East, in the Balkans, in South America, in Eastern Europe, in Ireland, in Africa, in India … And after war, internationalism striving to re-organise, reconstruct, revive and recreate fractured states, peoples and economies. The twentieth century has seen economic and technological growth on an enormous scale. If you add space science to all of this, the scale and range of change in the past hundred years becomes mind-blowing!

Our task, however, is more modest: to look at some examples in our three major genre areas of twentieth-century literature in context. In order to avoid repetition, it will be useful to comment briefly on the *intellectual* history of the last hundred years as it has influenced literature in English, starting with *modernism* and concluding with *post-modernism*.

Modernism to Post-Modernism

Modernism is the term used to describe a powerful intellectual movement, emerging during the first three decades of the twentieth century, which was in reaction to earlier realist traditions in art and literature. This reaction was influenced not only by the trauma of world war, but also by new theories about the human mind and psyche (Sigmund Freud), by the Marxist revolution in Russia, and by Sir James Frazer's ground-breaking study of human development from 'magical through religious to scientific thought'.

Literature became non-realist and non-traditional in form and subject, highly experimental and self-conscious (i.e. 'I am writing a novel – notice my strategies'). Novelists experimented with different methods of narrative: for example, telling the story from many different points of view; using free association or 'stream of consciousness' to represent a character's thoughts; or fragmenting the narrative, leaving unfilled spaces and unanswered questions. Poets too abandoned traditional poetic forms and wrote in *free verse*; dramatists mixed symbolism with action and dealt directly with taboo subjects like drunkenness and sex. Most modernist writers worried about whether they could at the same time communicate personal (subjective) experience and represent physical reality (the objective world), and say what they really meant. This anxiety often led to feelings of *alienation*. As the century wore on through the Depression of the Thirties, and yet another World War, social changes turned the conservatism of the Fifties to the radicalism of the Sixties and Seventies. Some new '-isms' emerged such as *feminism, post-colonialism* and *Marxist criticism*, all of which affected writers (as well as the critics taking their literary temperatures).

In the last three decades of the twentieth century the term *post-modernism* has become as important, mysterious and misused as *modernism* was at the beginning of the century. Post-modernist writers tend to be populist, not elitist; playful rather than experimental; they tend to work *with* technology not against it, and to be more optimistic than pessimistic. They still use modernist literary strategies (e.g. multi-narrative), but tend to be less confrontational and more celebratory in their representations of 'reality'. We shall catch glimpses in our genre extracts in this chapter of these twentieth-century writers and their innovative strategies – and of course, we shall investigate their *contexts*.

ACTIVITY 49

Use the timeline in this chapter to choose your own decade, and pick out two major events to research. Compare notes with other people in your group and decide what *general* comments about the twentieth century can be made on the basis of everyone's evidence.

Part 1: Contextualising Poetry

Poetry in this century broadens its appeal, with larger audiences and an increasing diversity of poets writing in a variety of Englishes (e.g. American, Australian, Welsh, Jamaican, Scottish). A brief list might include:

South Africa (Roy Fuller, Jenni Couzyn)
Australia (Les Murray)
New Zealand (Fleur Adcock, Alan Curnow)
West Indies (Grace Nichols, Derek Walcott)
Canada (Margaret Atwood)
India (Vikram Seth)
America (Wallace Stevens, Sylvia Plath)
Wales (Dylan Thomas, R.S. Thomas, Gillian Clarke)
Ireland (Seamus Heaney, Paul Muldoon)
Scotland (Hugh MacDiarmid, Jackie Kay)

It has been a century of innovation in poetic forms and structure, subjects and style, with poets using strategies like *defamiliarisation* (i.e. surprising the reader with the unexpected, *deviating* from the norm) to convey their message. Poetry has even become a public art form – in the London Tube, on advertising hoardings, and on 'poetry trails' along city paths and pavements. Poetry competitions, poetry magazines, visiting poets in schools, law offices – even the Navy has a ship's poet! Poetry is moving from an exclusive, rather elitist art form into something many people find fun, accessible, moving, inspiriting and comforting. Its context is the world and the experiences of the world, joyful or tragic, in a way we have not seen before.

a Ezra Pound (1885–1972)

Ezra Pound was a hugely influential figure in the development in English poetry in the early twentieth century, supporting and criticising in equal measure poets as diverse as the Imagist poet HD (Hilda Doolittle), Robert Frost and T.S. Eliot. Born and educated in America, he was an expert in European mediaeval literature who was also fascinated by Chinese literature. Some of his more extremist economic views led him into the dangerous waters of anti-semitism.

From Hugh Selwyn Mauberley (1920)

IV

These fought in any case,
and some believing,
            pro domo, in any case . . .
Some quick to arm,
some for adventure,
some from fear of weakness,
some from fear of censure,
some for love of slaughter, in imagination,
learning later . . .
some in fear, learning love of slaughter;

Died some, pro patria,
            non 'dulce' non 'et decor'. . .
walked eye-deep in hell
believing old men's lies, then unbelieving
came home, home to a lie,
home to many deceits,
home to old lies and new infamy;
usury age-old and age-thick
and liars in public places.

Daring as never before, wastage as never before.
Young blood and high blood,
fair cheeks, and fine bodies;

fortitude as never before

frankness as never before,
disillusions as never told in the old days,
hysterias, trench confessions,
laughter out of dead bellies

V
There died a myriad,
And of the best, among them,

For an old bitch gone in the teeth,
For a botched civilisation,
Charm, smiling at the good mouth,
Quick eyes gone under earth's lid
For two gross of broken statues,
For a few thousand battered books.

This is part of a sequence published in 1920 by this maverick scholar, poet and editor, as his critique of Western civilisation (**context of text**). From 1908 he lived in Europe, teaching, publishing poems and articles, founding the Imagist school of poets, and encouraging poets like T.S. Eliot to experiment with free verse (*vers libre*), concrete language and 'exact' imagery (**context of production**). Eliot famously dedicated *The Waste Land* (1925) to Pound, whom he called 'il miglior fabbro' (the greater master). *Hugh Selwyn Mauberley* (a fictional creation) is a sequence of 18 poems, which Pound himself describes as 'a farewell to London', but is much more personal and painful than this suggests. His divided persona, Mauberley, looks back at his struggles to be creative in an aesthetically bankrupt society.

The section quoted here looks back to the horror of the First World War and the tragic effects Pound and Eliot describe i.e. the fragmentation of civilised society (**context of cultural reference**). Pound makes use of the strategy of *intertextuality* (**context of text**) in his deliberately incomplete quotation from the Latin poet, Horace (*dulce et decorum est pro patria mori* ['it is sweet and fitting to die for one's country']); he is also alluding to Wilfred Owen's sarcastic use of the same quotation in his poem about the war ('the old lie'). Pound was not himself involved in the war, but several of his close friends died in the trenches, including a highly promising young sculptor ('for two gross of broken statues') and a poet and writer ('for a few thousand battered books').

How did people read this poem (**context of reception**)? In the immediate post-war period when society was in tatters, with a whole generation virtually wiped out, the audience for poetry (and experimental poetry) must have been a relatively small one, perhaps rather elitist. But Pound's sharp retrospective account of the war reflects everything his audience would recognise (the mixed emotions of volunteers in 1914, the realities of trench warfare, the criminal incompetence of the generals and their lies). Later, more literary responses from T.S. Eliot (1929), and F.R. Leavis (1932) are enthusiastic ('a great poem', 'documentary of an epoch', 'quintessential autobiography').

ACTIVITY 50

Read the extract on page 99 carefully and answer the following questions:

a Identify the words, phrases, images and poetic forms which convey Pound's attitudes to war.

b How do you respond as a twenty-first-century reader to this poetic representation of war?

c To what extent is the poem is limited by its historic context (**context of immediate situation**) for modern readers?

b W.H. Auden (1907–1973)

One of the great English poets of the twentieth century, Auden's poetry reflects his passion for social justice, his strong aesthetic and romantic sense, as well as his technical virtuosity.

Musee des Beaux Arts (1940)

About suffering they were never wrong,
The Old Masters: how well they understood
Its human position; how it takes place
While someone else is eating or opening a window or just
                              walking dully along;

How, when the aged are reverently, passionately waiting
For the miraculous birth, there always must be
Children who did not specially want it to happen, skating
On a pond at the edge of the wood:
They never forgot
That even the dreadful martyrdom must run its course
Anyhow in a corner, some untidy spot
Where the dogs go on with their doggy
                              life and the torturer's horse
Scratches its innocent behind on a tree.

In Brueghel's *Icarus*, for example: how everything turns away
Quite leisurely from the disaster; the ploughman may
Have heard the splash, the forsaken cry,
But for him it was not an important failure; the sun shone
As it had to on the white legs disappearing into the green
Water; and the expensive delicate ship that must have seen
Something amazing, a boy falling out of the sky,
Had somewhere to get to and sailed calmly on.

This poem was written from Brussels at the beginning of World War 2 (**context of production**). Auden had seen the special Pieter Breughel (1520–1569) alcove at the Musee Royaux des Beaux Arts, and alludes to three of the paintings there. The subject of the poem is the terrifying normality of disaster, and the fact that one person's tragedy is out of the frame for someone else, or may even be deliberately ignored (**context of text**). (It presents the opposite view from the one we heard earlier from John Donne 'No man is an island entire of itself – every man's death diminishes me, because I am part of mankind'). Auden establishes that we are in a world of visual art immediately, both by the poem's title and by the reference to 'Old Masters' (in other worlds, famous artists from the past), and although the theme of the poem is 'suffering', we need to unpick the art historical allusion (**context of cultural reference**). The central painting represents the Greek legend of Icarus, the young son of the master craftsman Daedalus. His father crafted wings for them both, secured by wax, but Icarus flew too near to the sun, the wax melted and he fell to his death. The story has been often used subsequently to symbolise the dangers of over-ambition. The other paintings alluded to, also by Breughel, are *The Numbering at Bethlehem* and *The Massacre of the Innocents* – both paintings on the subject of the vulnerability of youth. Auden chooses comic detail ('doggy life', 'torturer's horse') to contrast the normality of life going on in its usual down-to-earth way, whilst amazing things are happening. The tone is deceptively casual and laconic, the irregular lines sounding conversational rather than poetic.

Auden's technical skills in achieving this tone characterise his work as a whole. The reader has two different perspectives: that of the Old Masters, whose cool, distanced view of events is unruffled by pain; and that of the twentieth-century guilty observer – or author – of human suffering (**contexts of reception and of immediate situation**). This poem has always been popular (though not as famous as the poem 'Stop all the clocks, cut off the telephone' used in the film *Four Weddings and a Funeral*).

ACTIVITY 51

Below are listed a number of 'readings' of the poem, *Musee des Beaux Arts*. Your task is to choose *one* and argue the case *for* or *against* it.

a *Art historical reading* – the poem symbolises the danger of over-reaching ambition.
b *Marxist/political reading* – this is how we deal with disturbance in the hierarchic social order – ignore it.

c *Feminist reading* – everything that happens here takes place in a strictly patriarchal world, and no-one told Icarus not to go off with his father and do dangerous things.

c   Sujata Bhatt (1956–)

Bhatt is an Indian poet who currently lives in Europe.

Green Amber in Riga (for Gunnar Cirulis) (2001)

The woman on the street corner
was selling necklaces
            made of green amber.

Soon everywhere we turned
someone was selling amber:
necklaces, bracelets, nuggets with insects
            trapped inside –
But it was the green amber
that seemed closest to the sea
as if it had just been pulled
            out yesterday –

It was the raw texture
            of the green amber
I thought of, Gunnar,
as we sat in your house
and you poured the sap from birch trees
            into our glasses –

You pointed out the window
your uncle liked to look out of –

the room your father
            used to work in.
'This was our home – this was
our home …' you kept on
repeating with such joy –
your feet emphatic on the floor.
Your family home
taken over by the Red Army
and used so long
as officers' living quarters –
Your family home suddenly
returned to you, empty –
your childhood returned to you
            in your old age.

This poem, published in *The Forward Book of Poetry 2001*, is one of a short-listed group of poems submitted for the Forward Poetry Prizes 2000 by a range of poets (**context of production**). The chairman of the judges writes in the Foreword 'Whatever you expect from poetry – mind music, rinsed-out language, rhythmic excitement, wisdom, space-age narratives, sacred mysteries – you'll find it here', and confidently asserts that this anthology 'represents all that is best in British poetry'. In this context of competition, Bhatt's poem has been selected because it demonstrates so well how British poetry has evolved during this century. The clarity of tone, flexibility of line length, precision of description, focusing of emotion and climactic structure all characterise much late twentieth-century poetry (**context of text**). Starting with the image of green amber, the poet adds images of the sea, birch trees, and glasses before focusing on the 'real subject', the linking of Gunnar's childhood and age in the survival of her family home. The **context of cultural reference** includes the history and geography of Northern Europe in the twentieth century: Riga is the capital of Latvia, formerly part of the USSR (hence the reference to the Soviet Red Army). Because this poem is so recent, the **context of reception** and the **context of immediate situation** are inseparable – the reader is likely to empathise both with the poetic voice and with Gunnar, though the degree of empathy may depend on the reader's own generation.

ACTIVITY 52

Both the Auden and the Bhatt poems make significant use of *visual* detail (the Breughel paintings, the green amber) to communicate their meanings. Looking back at any twentieth-century poems you have read or studied, choose *one* or *two* to re-read. How important is selective visual detail in your poems? Is this a twentieth-century way of establishing contextual concreteness in modern poetry?

Unseen poem

Piccadilly Line

Girls, dressed for dancing,
board the tube at Earl's Court,
flutter, settle.
Chattering, excited by a vision
of glitter, their fragile bodies
carry invisible antennae,
missing nothing.
Faces velvet with bright camouflage,
they're unsung young stars – so young
it's thrilling just to be away from home.

One shrieks, points, springs away.
She's seen a moth
caught in the blonde strands
of her companion's hair,
a moth, marked
with all the shadow colours of blonde.
The friend's not scared;
gently she shakes her head,
tumbles it, dead,
into her hands.

At Piccadilly Circus they take flight,
skimming the escalator,
brushing past the collector,
up to the lure of light.

ACTIVITY 53

The unseen poem is by Carole Satyamurti, and was published in 1990. Read it carefully, and working in pairs, answer the following questions:

a What makes this a characteristically twentieth-century poem?

b How many modernist/post-modernist features (cf page 97) can you identify?

Part 2: Contextualising Literary Prose

In the course of the past hundred or so years, the novel and short story have reflected the seismic changes in society world-wide, both in terms of subject-matter, form and language.

Post-colonial writers:
V.S. Naipaul (*House for Mr Biswas*)
Vikram Seth (*A Suitable Boy*)
Nadine Gordimer (*The Conservationist*)
James Ngugi (*Petals of Blood*)

Chinua Achebe (*Things Fall Apart*)
Patrick White (*Voss*)
Peter Carey (*Oscar and Lucinda*)
F. Scott Fitzgerald (*Tender is the Night*)
William Faulkner (*Light in August*)
Margaret Atwood (*Alias Grace*)
Robertson Davies (*What's Bred in the Bone*)

There have been experimental novels (James Joyce *Finnegans Wake*, *Ulysses*), social comedy (Malcolm Bradbury *The History Man*), black comedy (Martin Amis *London Fields*), magic realism (Angela Carter *Wise Children*, *The Bloody Chamber*) and social history (William Golding *Rites of Passage*). Women writers are as active and successful as in the nineteenth-century – perhaps more so. Certainly some of the most innovative and exciting writers are female, from Toni Morrison and Iris Murdoch to Zadie Smith and Barbara Kingsolver. Fiction remains popular with the general public in all its generic manifestations, from science fiction and detective stories to 'Aga sagas' (Joanna Trollope's stories about rural middle-class *angst*) and Mills and Boon romance. The appeal of storytelling is as powerful as ever, and publishers are endlessly keen to please their audiences by offering very substantial financial advances to favoured writers and encouraging the literary celebrity culture, with its well-publicised annual award ceremonies (ranging from the Booker to the Whitbread and the Orange prizes). It seems likely that the novel will continue to retain its current pole position over the *next* hundred years.

a Katherine Mansfield (1888–1923)

The New Zealand writer spent her most creative years in Europe, but nevertheless found her childhood experiences a rich resource for some of her best short stories. A close friend of D.H. Lawrence and his wife Frieda, she was part of the English literary establishment – like Lawrence, she died prematurely of tuberculosis.

From At the Bay (1922)

Very early morning. The sun was not yet risen, and the whole of Crescent Bay was hidden under a white sea-mist. The big bush-covered hills at the back were smothered. You could not see where they ended and the paddocks and bungalows began. The sandy road was gone ... there were no white dunes covered with reddish grass beyond them; there was nothing to mark which was beach and where was sea. A heavy dew had fallen.
The grass was blue. Big drops hung on the bushes and just did not fall; the silvery fluffy toi-toi was limp on its long stalks, and all the marigolds and pinks in the bungalow gardens were bowed to the earth with wetness. It looked as though the sea had beaten up softly in the darkness, as though one immense wave had come rippling, rippling – how far? Perhaps if you had wakened in the middle of the night you might have seen a big fish flicking in at the window and gone again ....
Round the corner of Crescent Bay, between the piled up masses of broken rock, a flock of sheep came pattering. They were huddled together, a small, tossing, woolly mass, and their thin stick-like legs trotted along quickly as if the cold and the quiet

had frightened them. Behind them an old sheep-dog, his soaking paws covered with sand, ran along with his nose to the ground, but carelessly, as if thinking of something else. . . . The sheep ran forwards in little pattering rushes; they began to bleat, and ghostly flocks and herds answered them from under the sea. 'Baa! Baaa!' And now big spots of light gleamed in the mist . . . The sun was rising. It was marvellous how quickly the mist thinned, sped away, dissolved from the shallow plain, rolled up from the bush and was gone as if in a hurry to escape . . . Now the leaping glittering sea was so bright it made one's eyes ache to look at it. . . . [The sheep] were just clear of the summer colony before the first sleeper turned over and lifted a drowsy head; their cry sounded in the dreams of little children . . . who lifted up their arms to drag down, to cuddle the darling little woolly lambs of sleep. . . . The breeze of morning lifted in the bush and the smell of leaves and wet black earth mingled with the sharp smell of the sea . . .

II

A few moments later the back door of one of the bungalows opened, and a figure in a broad-striped bathing-suit flung down the paddock, cleared the stile, rushed through the tussock grass into the hollow, staggered up the sandy hillock, and raced for dear life over the big porous stones, over the cold, wet pebbles, on to the hard sand that gleamed like oil. Splish-Splosh! Splish-Splosh! The water bubbled round his legs as Stanley Burnell waded out exulting. First man in as usual! He'd beaten them all again. And he swooped down to souse his head and neck.
'Hail, brother! All hail, Thou Mighty One!' A velvety bass voice came booming over the water.
    Great Scott! Damnation take it! Stanley lifted up to see a dark head bobbing far out and an arm lifted. It was Jonathan Trout – there before him! 'Glorious morning!' sang the voice.
'Yes, very fine!' said Stanley briefly. Why the dickens didn't the fellow stick to his part of the sea?'

These two edited sections (**context of text**) form part of a sequence of stories narrating the experiences of a New Zealand family moving house from the city to the seaside (from Wellington to Palliser Bay). Based on Mansfield's own childhood (**context of production**), the stories are told from multiple perspectives: that of the children (Kezia and Lottie), Beryl, the younger sister of Linda Burnell, Linda herself, her husband Stanley, and her elderly mother.

In the first section Mansfield is creating an impressionistic word picture of the dawn over the bay, the sounds, colours and textures of the experience. Modernist overtones include the references to dreams, and the constantly shifting and dissolving images of mist and vapour. In the second section this dreamy, evanescent world is interrupted by Stanley Burnell's vigorous early morning swim ('Splish-Splosh!). Burnell's engaging but difficult personality is skilfully conveyed by the semi-serious, semi-comic description of his actions and words, probably reflecting Mansfield's own ambiguous feelings about her own father (**context of text**). The world of prosperous city commuters in this idyllic landscape is only lightly sketched here, but there is an evident contrast between the rural workers and Stanley and his ironic business colleague Jonathan Trout (**context of cultural reference**). New Zealand society at this date (late nineteenth/early twentieth century) was relatively isolated and inward-looking, secure in its comfortable provincialism (though Mansfield never denies the reality of pain as well as happiness in human relationships).

Contemporary readers of Mansfield's short story collections (*In a German Pension* 1911, *Bliss and Other Stories* 1920, *The Garden Party and Other Stories* 1922) admired her work greatly (**context of reception**); Virginia Woolf even remarked 'I was jealous of her writing. The only writing I have ever been jealous of.' Mansfield's painterly skill in choosing the telling detail makes her writing vivid and sensuous; she combines this with a powerfully ironic perspective on human behaviour. Her descriptions of adult experience from a child's perspective are particularly effective. A modern reader (**context of immediate situation**) might find the social environment difficult to access, but reading from the feminist position works well with Mansfield.

ACTIVITY 54

Write the opening paragraph of a short story in the style of Katherine Mansfield.

b Ralph Ellison (1914–1994)

Ellison wrote this ground-breaking novel (both in terms of its subject matter and form) as a highly educated African-American in the Fifties who had experienced for himself the overt and covert racism of pre-Civil Rights America.

From Invisible Man (1952)

I am an invisible man. No, I am not a spook like those who haunted Edgar Allan Poe; nor am I one of your Hollywood-movie ectoplasms. I am a man of substance, of flesh and bone, fibre and liquids – and I might even be said to possess a mind. I am invisible, understand, simply because people refuse to see me. Like the bodiless heads you see sometimes in circus side-shows, it is as though I have been surrounded by mirrors of hard distorting glass. When they approach me they see only my surroundings, themselves, or figments of their imagination – indeed, everything and anything except me.

Nor is my invisibility exactly a matter of bio-chemical accident to my epidermis. That invisibility to which I refer occurs because of a peculiar disposition of the eyes of those with whom I come in contact. A matter of the construction of their *inner* eyes, those eyes with which they look through their physical eyes upon reality. I am not complaining, nor am I protesting either. It is sometimes advantageous to be unseen, although it is most often rather wearing on the nerves. Then too, you're constantly being bumped against by those of poor vision. Or again, you often doubt if you really exist. You wonder whether you aren't simply a phantom in other people's minds. Say, a figure in a nightmare which a sleeper tries with all his strength to destroy. It's when you feel like this that, out of resentment, you begin to bump people back. And, let me confess, you feel that way most of the time. You ache with the need to convince yourself that you do exist in the real world, that you're a part of all the sound and anguish, and you strike out with your fists, you curse and you swear to make them recognise you. And, alas, it's seldom successful.

The title of this novel had been used before (*The Invisible Man* by H.G. Wells 1897), though Ellison's novel about black-white relations in mid-fifties America, and the search for the self, is very different from Wells's science fiction romance (**context of text**). Nevertheless the *idea* of invisibility symbolises perfectly the experience of African-Americans at the time. This 'invisibility' reflected the conscious refusal of white American society to *see* the social, economic, educational, political and personal injustice experienced by black American citizens (**context of cultural reference**). In this extract Ellison analyses the nature of this invisibility, using the narrative voice of the unnamed hero to explore the nature of sight and seeing. Ellison's techniques are characteristically modernist, breaking up the conventions of narrative structure, and addressing the reader directly, *requiring* him or her to assess their position in the context of black-white relations (**context of immediate situation**). The hero's acute self-awareness reflects the influence of existential philosophy (with its emphasis on the individual as source of all value). This is complicated by the debt Ellison owes to the German writer Kafka and his tormented, isolated and alienated heroes (**context of text**).

How did the contemporary audience respond to *Invisible Man* (**context of reception**)? Despite the fact that it probably made uncomfortable reading for many people, the novel was immediately successful, and has remained so. Though Ellison produced other writing, his high reputation rests on this one novel. Modern readers (**context of immediate situation**), attuned to the complexities of racist attitudes and behaviour, though *reading from non-racist positions* are likely to respond within the context of individual experience. The concept of invisibility as a metaphor for racism retains its validity even in the early twenty-first century.

c Julian Barnes (1946–)

Barnes's novels reflect his constant awareness of new possibilities for the writer of fiction. They range from the prize-winning *Flaubert's Parrot* (1994) which combines self-analysis with biographical detection and literary criticism, to the success and failure of relationships (*Talking it Over* 1991) and death and aging (*Staring at the Sun* 1992). He often adopts an ironic, even satirical stance in relation to his subjects.

From A History of the World in 10½ Chapters (1989)

As far as we were concerned the whole business of the Voyage began when we were invited to report to a certain place by a certain time. That was the first we heard of the scheme. We didn't know anything of the political background. God's wrath with his creation was news to us; we just got caught up in it willy-nilly. *We* weren't in any way to blame (you don't really believe that story about the serpent, do you? – it was just Adam's black propaganda), and yet the consequences for us were equally severe: every species wiped out except a single breeding pair, and that couple consigned to the high seas under the charge of an old rogue with a drink problem who was already in the seventh century of his life.
So the word went out; but characteristically they didn't tell us the truth. Did you imagine that in the vicinity of Noah's palace (oh, he wasn't poor, that Noah) there dwelt a convenient example of every species on earth? Come, come. No, they were obliged to advertise, and then select the best pair that presented itself. Since they didn't want to cause a universal panic, they announced a competition for twosomes – a sort of beauty contest cum brains trust cum Darby-and-Joan event – and told

contestants to present themselves at Noah's gate by a certain month. You can imagine the problems. For a start, not everyone has a competitive nature, so perhaps only the grabbiest turned up. Animals who weren't smart enough to read between the lines felt they simply didn't need to win a luxury cruise for two, all expenses paid, thank you very much. Nor had Noah and his staff allowed for the fact that some species hibernate at a given time of year; let alone the obvious fact that certain animals travel more slowly than others. There was a particularly relaxed sloth, for instance – an exquisite creature, I can vouch for it personally – which had scarcely got down to the foot of its tree before it was wiped out in the great wash of God's vengeance. What do you call that – natural selection? I'd call it professional incompetence.

This extract is taken from 'The Stowaway', the first chapter of this remarkable book (**context of text**), which consistently overturns reader expectations in terms of subject, narrative method and hidden meanings. The title *A History of the World in 10½ Chapters* is itself disconcerting, in that it challenges our ideas about fictional structure – and much more importantly, mischievously suggests that the vastness and complexity of 'the world' can be neatly parcelled up into neat and tidy sections. The dominant tone of irony is immediately established. What holds the ten chapters together is that they are all variant narratives or accounts of shipwreck and survival; the 'half' (called Parenthesis) is a meditation on human love, also subject to upheavals and rescues. 'The Stowaway' tells the story of Noah's Ark from an insider's point of view – the narrator (whose identity we don't discover till the final page of the chapter) reveals all. At an *intertextual* level Barnes uses Genesis for his particular purposes, adapting, extending and embroidering on the original story. What makes it work – and makes it comic – is the juxtaposition between the solemn Biblical events (God punishing corrupt and sinful humanity with universal drowning) and the down-to-earth, businesslike quality of the narrative voice, sharing his thoroughly twentieth-century interpretation of all the goings on with the astonished reader. Barnes's irony is so pervasive that the reader is almost forced into a similar position (**contexts of immediate situation and reception**). The narrator actually plays with other possible readings of the events he recounts (feminist, post-modernist, Marxist) but persuades us to adopt the Barnesian irony.

Barnes is a clever writer (**context of production**), a journalist who has also worked in the precise world of dictionary-making (lexicography). He is perfectly at home with the ordinariness of everyday existence and equally comfortable with art history, mediaeval legal documents and metaphysics. His humour and delight in the absurd are applied across the range of his subject matter, and engage our response almost irresistably. He works within a social framework (**context of cultural reference**) which is instantly recognisable – certainly to a late twentieth-century audience, and probably to twenty-first-century readers too. The popularity of the book on publication was considerable (it has been an A Level English Literature text!), and is likely to continue.

Look back at the three literary prose extracts. You will remember that in Chapter 3 (page 38), we differentiated between *lisible* (readerly) and *scriptible* (writerly) texts. Your task is to decide which term (readerly or writerly) best describes these three passages, and to select three examples from *each extract* which supports your choice of term.

Unseen literary prose

The whole business of French opened a new world to Francis. Of course he had noticed that a lot of people in Blairlogie spoke this language, with varying degrees of elegance, but he now discovered that the hardware store kept by somebody called Dejordo was, in reality, the property of Emile Desjardins, and that the Legarry family were, to those who spoke French, Legarè. Some tact had to be exercised here, because it was a point of honour among the English-speaking populace to mispronounce any French name, as a rebuke to those who were so foolish, and probably sneaky and disloyal as well, as to speak a private lingo. But Francis was a quick boy – 'gleg in the uptake' as his Scots grandfather put it – and he learned not only two kinds of French, but two kinds of English as well. In the schoolyard a substantial quantity of anything whatever was always described beyond what could be covered on foot was 'a fur piece of a ways'. When adults greeted one another with 'Fine day, eh!', the proper reply was 'Fine day altogether'. He mastered all these niceties with the same ease with which he digested his food and grew, and by the time he was nine he was not merely bilingual, but multilingual, and could talk to anybody he met in their own language, be it French, patois, Canadian-Scots English, or the speech of the Upper Ottawa Valley.

The extract above comes from a novel published in 1985. What deductions can you make about its *contexts of text, production, cultural reference,* and *immediate situation*?

Part 3: Contextualising Drama

Drama in the twentieth century has flourished as much – or even more – than in earlier periods in England and America, as well as in other post-colonial cultures. Predictably, the radical changes in society are reflected in this most direct and fluid of art forms. There have been a whole range of changes in the writing and the production of plays in this period, with much experimentation. For example, the naturalism of late nineteenth-century European theatre (e.g. Ibsen) evolved into something more symbolic, impressionistic and modernist; nevertheless, a powerful strand of realism was retained both in English and American theatre. More socially challenging subject-matter emerged, from arms dealing and prostitution (Shaw's *Major Barbara* 1905, *Mrs Warren's Profession* 1902), to the effects of drug addiction on the family (Eugene O'Neill, *Long Day's Journey into*

Night 1940–41). Indeed, theatre became an even more powerful vehicle for social criticism as the century matured, with a wide variety of experimental staging and acting strategies developing. Key influences on twentieth-century drama include Japanese Noh theatre (use of masks, music), German Expressionism (non-realistic, almost surreal style), Brecht's politicised social realism, Stanislavski's Method acting theory (derived from his work at the Moscow Art Theatre), the Theatre of the Absurd (Samuel Beckett and Jean Genet) and the Theatre of Cruelty (Antonin Artaud).

Major American dramatists include: Eugene O'Neill (*The Emperor Jones* 1920, *Mourning becomes Electra* 1931), Thornton Wilder (*Our Town* 1938), Lillian Hellman (*The Little Foxes* 1939), Arthur Miller (*Death of a Salesman* 1949, *The Crucible* 1953), Tennessee Williams (*The Glass Menagerie* 1945, *A Streetcar Named Desire* 1947), Edward Albee (*The Zoo Story* 1958, *Who's Afraid of Virginia Woolf?* 1962), and David Mamet (*Glengarry Glen Ross* 1983, *Oriana* 1995).

Irish dramatists include: J.M. Synge who wrote about the struggles of the poor in *Riders to the Sea* (1904) and *The Playboy of the Western World* (1907); as did Sean O'Casey (*Juno and the Paycock* 1924, *The Plough and the Stars* 1926), Brendan Behan (*The Hostage* 1958) and Brian Friel (*Translations* 1980). Most radical of all in technique and subject was Samuel Beckett (*Waiting for Godot* 1955, *Endgame* 1958). Beckett influenced **English** playwrights like Harold Pinter (*The Caretaker* 1960), Tom Stoppard (*Rosencrantz and Guildenstern are Dead* 1966, *Arcadia* 1993), and the radical **South African** dramatist Athol Fugard.

Prior to Beckett, the English theatre in the early half of the century lacked the vigour and dynamism of American theatre, although there were interesting individual plays like Noel Coward's *The Vortex* (1924) or the verse drama of Christopher Fry and T.S. Eliot. It isn't until the late fifties that English theatre is re-invigorated by the social realism 'slice of life' plays by John Osborne (*Look Back in Anger* 1960, *Luther* 1961) and Arnold Wesker (*Chicken Soup With Barley* 1958, *Roots* 1959, *I'm Talking about Jerusalem* 1960), as well as plays like *A Day In the Life of Joe Egg* (1967) by Peter Nichols and Joe Orton's *What the Butler Saw* (1969). English dramatists of the seventies, eighties and nineties include Peter Schaffer (*Equus* 1973), Alan Ayckbourn (*The Norman Conquests* 1974) Howard Brenton (*Romans in Britain* 1980), David Hare (*Racing Demon* 1990, *Murmuring Judges* 1991, *The Absence of War* 1993), David Edgar (*Pentecost* 1994), Michael Frayn (*Copenhagen* 1999) as well as Caryl Churchill (*Cloud Nine* 1979, *Top Girls* 1982).

Lists can seem tedious, but it's important to recognise that the twentieth century has been a remarkable period for drama. As a medium it has mirrored the traumas and upheavals of the age, has challenged, cheered, encouraged, angered, moved, annoyed and inspired its audiences. At its very best, it makes us think, and keep on thinking, long after the play is over.

a Eugene O'Neill (1888–1953)

O'Neill was the son of a famous New York actor. After a variety of career changes (seaman, gold prospector, journalist, actor) he formed an association with an experimental theatre company, the Provincetown Players (Massachusetts). The first plays he wrote for the company all drew on his own experience as a seaman; these included *Bound East for Cardiff* (1916), *The Moon of the Caribbees* (1918) and *The Emperor Jones* (1920). Twenty years later O'Neill's remarkable *Long Day's Journey into Night* (1940–41) was a thinly disguised account of his own family tragedy (ex-actor father [Tyrone], morphine-addicted mother [Mary], two sons [Jamie and Edmund], one a hard-drinker, the other a journalist with a potentially serious illness).

From Long Day's Journey into Night (produced posthumously in 1956)

Jamie I can't help being suspicious. Any more than you can. (*Bitterly*) That's the hell of it. And it makes it hell for Mama! She watches us watching her –
Tyrone (*sadly*) I know. (*Tensely*) Well, what was it? Can't you speak out?
Jamie Nothing, I tell you. Just my damned foolishness. Around three o'clock this morning I woke up and heard her moving around the spare room. Then she went to the bathroom. I pretended to be asleep. She stopped in the hall to listen, as if she wanted to make sure I was.
Tyrone (*with forced scorn*) For God's sake, is that all? She told me herself the foghorn kept her awake all night, and every night since Edmund's been sick she's been up and down, going to his room to see how he was.
Jamie (*eagerly*) Yes, that's right, she did stop to listen outside his room. (*Hesitantly again*) It was her being in the spare room again that scared me. I couldn't help remembering that when she starts sleeping alone there, it has always been a sign –
Tyrone It isn't this time! It's easily explained. Where else could she go last night to get away from my snoring? (*he gives way to a burst of resentful anger*) By God, how you can live with a mind that sees nothing but the worst motives behind everything is beyond me!
Jamie (*stung*) Don't pull that! I've just said I was all wrong. Don't you suppose that I'm as glad of that as you are!
Tyrone (*mollifyingly*) I'm sure you are, Jamie. (*A pause. His expression becomes sombre. He speaks slowly with a superstitious dread*) it would be like a curse she can't escape if worry over Edmund – It was after her long sickness after bringing him into the world that she first –
Jamie She didn't have anything to do with it!
Tyrone I'm not blaming her.
Jamie (*bitingly*) Then who are you blaming? Edmund, for being born?
Tyrone You damned fool! No one was to blame.
Jamie That bastard of a doctor was! From what Mama's said, he was another cheap quack like Hardy! You wouldn't pay for a first-rate –
Tyrone That's a lie! (*Furiously*) So I'm to blame! That's what you're driving at, is it? You evil-minded loafer!

This play is quite overtly autobiographical: O'Neill dedicated 'this play of old sorrow, written in tears and blood' to his wife, Carlotta, as a tribute to her 'love and tenderness which gave me the faith in love that enabled me to face my dead at last and write ... with deep pity and understanding and forgiveness for *all* the four haunted Tyrones' (**context of production**).

O'Neill himself was the tormented younger brother who is named but does not appear in this extract. Indeed, when he wrote the play, O'Neill intended that it should only be produced after his death.

Throughout his remarkable career (he was awarded the Nobel Prize for Literature in 1936) O'Neill proved to be an endlessly original writer, ranging from the early naturalistic plays about prostitution on the New York waterfront or the rise and fall of a West Indian 'emperor' figure (*Anna Christie*, *The Emperor Jones*) to the reworked *Oresteia* in *Mourning becomes Electra*, and the brilliantly observed tragedy *The Iceman Cometh*. He experimented with everything from Expressionism to Naturalism and the 'stream of consciousness technique' to convey his ideas about 'self-destruction, self-deception and redemption'. O'Neill's plays are predominantly tragic, and this version of his own family's sufferings has the predictable tragic ending (**context of text**). O'Neill manages to convey his characters' changing emotions and relationships with each other through his ear for convincing dialogue, and subtle use of symbolism (the foghorn in the bay). Finally produced in 1956, *Long Day's Journey into Night* was a great success (**context of reception**): subsequent productions have confirmed its tragic power to move a variety of audiences (**context of immediate situation**), probably because the theme of destructive family love has universal resonance, despite its specific location in the typically American world of second-generation immigrants, social isolation and alcoholism (**context of cultural reference**).

b Harold Pinter (1930–)

Born and educated in the East End of London, Pinter started to publish poetry before he was twenty. He then became a professional actor, until the publication and performance of his first play, *The Room* (1957). This was rapidly followed by *The Birthday Party* (1958) and *The Caretaker* (1960). In *The Caretaker* there are three characters: Davies (an older, casual worker) and two younger men (Mick and Aston, late twenties/early thirties), who are apparently brothers. The whole action takes place in a cluttered, crowded bed-sitting room, part of a larger house. This extract is from Act 1.

From The Caretaker (1960)

Davies Did you see what happened with that one?
Aston I only got the end of it.
Davies Comes up to me, parks a bucket of rubbish at me, tells me to take it out the back. It's not my job to take out the bucket! They got a boy there for taking out the bucket. I wasn't engaged to take out buckets. My job's cleaning the floor, clearing up the tables, doing a bit of washing-up, nothing to do with taking out buckets!
Aston Uh. [*he crosses . . . to get the electric toaster*]
Davies (*following*) Yes, well say I had! Even if I had! Even if I was supposed to take the bucket out, who was this git to come up and give me orders? We got the same standing. He's not my boss. He's nothing superior to me.
Aston What was he, a Greek?
Davies Not him, he was Scotch. He was a Scotchman. [*Aston goes back to his bed with the toaster and starts to unscrew the plug. Davies follows him*] You got an eye of him, didn't you?

Aston Yes.

Davies I told him what to do with his bucket. Didn't I? You heard. Look here, I said, I'm an old man, I said, where I was brought up we had some idea how to talk to old people with the proper respect, we was brought up with the right ideas, if I had a few years off me I'd ... I'd break you in half. That was after the guvnor give me the bullet. Making too much commotion, he says. Commotion, me! Look here, I said to him, I got my rights. I told him that. I might have been on the road but nobody's got more rights than I have. Let's have a bit of fair play, I said. Anyway, he give me the bullet. [*he sits in the chair*] That's the sort of place. [*Pause*] If you hadn't come out and stopped that Scotch git I'd be inside the hospital now. I'd have cracked my head on that pavement if he'd have landed. I'll get him. One night I'll get him. When I find myself around that direction. [*Aston crosses to the plug box to get another plug*] I wouldn't mind so much but I left all my belongings in that place, in the back room there. All of them, the lot there was, you see, in this bag. Every lousy blasted bit of all my bleeding belongings I left down there now. In the rush of it. I bet he's having a poke around in it now this very moment.

Aston I'll pop down sometime and pick them up for you. [*Aston goes back to his bed and starts to fix the plug on the toaster*]

Davies Anyway, I'm obliged to you, letting me ... letting me have a bit of a rest, like ... for a few minutes.

The whole play takes place in the same room (**context of text**), reflecting the influence of Samuel Beckett and the Theatre of the Absurd. This is demonstrated by the fact that Davies is a vagrant (cf the tramps in *Waiting for Godot* – an example of *intertextuality*) and by the nature of the 'action', which derives almost entirely from the responses of the three characters to their physical environment (the two beds, the window, the bucket under the leaking roof, the toaster, the electrolux). In this extract (early in Act 1) we find out about the situation which led Aston to invite Davies back to the room. Davies is eager to explain exactly what happened, Aston is only mildly interested. From his speech (**context of immediate situation**) we make our own judgement about Davies, noting his vulnerability, attempts at self-justification, seeming aggressiveness and lack of self-awareness. An audience in 1960 might have been surprised by the fact that the 'hero' is a vagrant, by the focus on trivial but faintly sinister action, and by Pinter's brilliant ear for colloquial language (**context of reception**). The social and cultural ambience in the early sixties was becoming radical and liberal, democratising literature and seeking 'truth' in unexpected places (**context of cultural reference**). Even so, *The Caretaker* was commercially as well as critically successful, and has continued to intrigue, amuse and disturb audiences. Pinter (**context of production**) has continued to write plays as well as scripts for film, radio and television, exploiting his remarkable skills in creating dialogue, and portraying jealousy, obsession and family conflict with overtones of menace and darkness.

ACTIVITY 57

If possible, read the two extracts from O'Neill and Pinter *aloud* to get the full flavour of the dialogue. Then, working in pairs, answer the following questions.

a Which text appeals to you more ? Give your reasons in as much detail as possible.

b What differences do you notice in the way each dramatist presents social class?

c In *The Caretaker* nothing much happens: in *Long Day's Journey into Night* the events are of major significance. What explanation can you suggest for this?

The extract from *Cloud Nine* by Caryl Churchill (on page 115) is from early in Act 1. The dramatist's purpose in each is similar – to establish key themes and relationships.

a What are these key themes and relationships in this play?

b How does the dramatist use the five contexts (*reception, production, text, cultural reference, immediate situation*) to achieve this? Give examples for each context.

Unseen drama

[*Low bright sun. Verandah with Union Jack*]

Betty: I thought you would never come. The day's so long without you.
Clive: Long ride in the bush.
Betty: Is anything wrong? I heard drums.
Clive: Nothing serious. Beauty is a damned good mare. I must get some new boots sent from home. These ones have never been right. I have a blister.
Betty: My poor dear foot.
Clive: It's nothing.
Betty: Oh but it's sore.
Clive: We are not in this country to enjoy ourselves. Must have ridden fifty miles. Spoke to three different headmen who would all gladly chop off each other's heads and wear them round their waists.
Betty: Clive!
Clive: Don't be squeamish, Betty, let me have my joke. And what has my little dove done today?
Betty: I've read a little.
Clive: Good. Is it good?
Betty: It's poetry.
Clive: You're so delicate and sensitive.
Betty: And I played the piano. Shall I send for the children?
Clive: Yes, in a minute. I've a piece of news for you.
Betty: Good news?
Clive: You'll certainly think it's good. A visitor.
Betty: From home?
Clive: No. Well of course originally from home.
Betty: Man or woman?
Clive: Man.
Betty: I can't imagine.
Clive: Something of an explorer. Bit of a poet. Odd chap but brave as a lion. And a great admirer of yours.
Betty: What do you mean? Whoever can it be?
Clive: With an H and a B. And does conjuring tricks for little Edward.
Betty: That sounds like Mr Bagley.
Clive: Harry Bagley.
Betty: He certainly doesn't admire me, Clive, what a thing to say. How could I possibly guess from that. He's hardly explored anything at all, he's just been up a river, he's done nothing at all compared with what you do. You should have said a heavy drinker and a bit of a bore.
Clive: But you like him well enough. You don't mind him coming?
Betty: Anyone at all to break the monotony.

Part 4: Contextualising Non-Literary Prose

Non-literary texts have proliferated throughout the period, especially in the fields of media, business and finance, science, social science, education, critical theory and medicine. The strong growth of new technologies has enabled spoken texts to be recorded and analysed, and a better understanding of linguistic strategies (and in particular rhetorical strategies) to evolve. Audiences have continued to expand as literacy increases, and more people have access to higher education. The strength of 'non-fiction' publishers' lists (noted weekly, monthly and yearly in the broadsheets) confirms the vitality and generic range of non-fictional prose today. All this despite the gloomy predictions of publishers and booksellers (not to speak of authors!).

a Franklin Delano Roosevelt (1882–1945)

The extract below is from the Inaugural Address of Franklin Roosevelt to an American people facing extremes of poverty and unemployment (the Great Depression) as a result of the Stock Exchange collapse of 1929. Despite his own privileged background (he was a distant cousin of President Theodore Roosevelt) the Democrat Franklin Roosevelt was an indefatigable reformer, on the side of the disadvantaged (and strongly anti-fascist during World War 2). He achieved all this in spite of serious and chronic health problems, the result of contracting the disabling illness poliomyelitis when he was just short of forty.

From the First Inaugural Address of Franklin Roosevelt (4 March 1933)

This is a day of national consecration, and I am certain that my fellow-Americans expect that on my induction into the Presidency I will address them with a candor and a decision which the present situation of our nation impels.
This is pre-eminently the time to speak the truth, the whole truth, frankly and boldly. Nor need we shrink from honestly facing conditions in our country today. This great nation will endure as it has endured, will revive and will prosper.
So first of all let me assert my firm belief that the only thing we have to fear is fear itself – nameless, unreasoning, unjustified terror which paralyzes needed efforts to convert retreat into advance.
In every dark hour of our national life a leadership of frankness and vigor has met with that understanding and support of the people themselves which is essential to victory. I am convinced that you will again give that support to leadership in these critical days.
In such a spirit on my part and on yours we face our common difficulties. They concern, thank God, only material things. Values have shrunken to fantastic levels; taxes have risen; our ability to pay has fallen, government of all kinds is faced by serious curtailment of income; the means of exchange are frozen in the currents of trade; the withered leaves of industrial enterprise lie on every side; farmers find no

markets for their produce; the savings of many years in thousands of families are gone.

More important, a host of unemployed citizens face the grim problem of existence, and an equally great number toil with little return. . .

Yet our distress comes from no failure of substance. . . Nature still offers her bounty and human efforts have multiplied it. Plenty is at our doorstep, but a generous use of it languishes at the very sight of the supply.

Primarily, this is because the rulers of the exchange of man's goods have failed through their own stubbornness and their own incompetence, have admitted that failure and have abdicated. Practices of the unscrupulous money changers stand indicted in the court of public opinion, rejected by the hearts and minds of men. . ..

They know only the rules of a generation of self-seekers.

They have no vision, and when there is no vision the people perish.

This Inaugural Address (though assisted by speech-writers) was definitely Roosevelt's own (**context of production**) – his style remains consistent despite changes in personnel among his speech-writers. Its purpose, of course, is to convince his audience that, as the new President, he will resolve the current economic crisis as far as he is able, relieve their distress, and deal with those responsible for it. He uses powerfully persuasive words and rhetorical strategies (**context of text**) to describe the present predicament of the American people, as well as figurative language and syntactic structures. At this moment it has been said that 'the depression was at its lowest ebb and the economic situation of the country on the verge of complete collapse' (**context of cultural frame of reference**). Roosevelt's policies were to focus on recovery, relief and reform, and indications of this can be found through out this extract. The address was enthusiastically received (**context of reception**) and remains famous not only for its content but also for its language. Historians and other readers today (**context of immediate situation**) may offer differing interpretations of the speech, depending on their theoretical stance. The text remains (even in an extracted form) an impressive example of political persuasion.

ACTIVITY 59

Roosevelt's address reveals a great deal about **a** his own purposes and **b** his understanding of his audience and their needs.

a Identify the words and phrases which indicate his understanding of his contemporary audience and their needs.

b How do you, as a twenty-first-century 'audience', respond to his persuasion? Working in pairs, go through the extract and decide which arguments still work today.

---

b Eric Newby (1919–)

Newby is a writer of wide-ranging skills and abilities, matching the extraordinary variety of his life. He sailed round Cape Horn as a young man, fought in World War 2 in different campaigns, was a prisoner of war in Italy, and then moved into the fashion business, followed by publishing and travel writing. This extract is taken from his account of an expedition into Northern Afghanistan taken with Hugh, a diplomat friend. The area of the Hindu Kush is north-east of Kabul.

From A Short Walk in the Hindu Kush (1958)

'What did they say?' Hugh asked [Abdul Ghiyas] when we were clear of [the band of Pathans].

'That there are robbers on the road between here and Parian who have just taken everything from a man travelling.'

A couple more miles and we came to a place where the river swirled round the base of a cliff and another torrent came racing down from the left to join it.

'*Ao Khawak*,' said Abdul Ghiyas, 'the meeting of the waters; where it comes in from the Khawak Pass. The way of Timur Leng.'

This was the place where Timur Leng's wild cavalry crossed the Hindu Kush on their way from the Oxus to India in 1398.

The bridge over the Khawak consisted of two parallel tree trunks, one higher than the other, with the gap between filled with rocks and turf. The trunks were loose and as we trod on them they rolled apart and chunks of rock and turf crashed into the torrent below . . . .

Beyond the river we found the traveller who had had everything taken from him. He was a young man of about twenty and he was lying face downwards in the shadow of a boulder with his skull smashed to pulp. Whoever had done it had probably struck him down while someone else had engaged him in conversation. The instrument was lying some yards away – a long splinter of rock with blood on it. He was only very recently dead.

'What do you think we should do?' Hugh asked Abdul Ghiyas. His suggestion was so eminently suitable that we adopted it.

'Let us leave immediately,' he said.

Above our heads hovered a large bearded vulture, a lammergeier, a whitish bird with brown wing markings. As we stood there it was joined by another.

'We call them "the burnt ones,"' said Abdul Ghiyas.

After placing a large flat stone over the head of the corpse we went on our way.

Now the road became even more desolate, the gorge narrower still, filled with a wild chaos of granite blocks ... High on the cliffs above where there were slabs of limestone, we could see the mouths of dark caves. Higher still granite cliffs overhung the track and from time to time a slab of granite would detach itself and fall with a clang into the gorge. It was no place to linger.

Yet down by the water's edge, wheat was growing in minute fields hemmed in by rocks, and the water sparkled as it ran swiftly in the irrigation ditches . . .

Finally ... we came out of the gorge. The valley broadened out; to the east the hills rolled back, covered in mustard-coloured grass like grass which has had snow on it. Beyond these hills a range of big jagged snow peaks rose up shimmering in the sun.

One of the purposes of travel writing (**context of text**) is to enable readers to experience places and conditions otherwise unfamiliar or inaccessible; another is to provide new perspectives on places that are already familiar; another is to earn a living for the travel writer (**context of production**). The genre of travel writing, as we have already seen, has ancient origins (oral narrative) and has always been popular with audiences. Whether travel writing *primarily* entertains or informs (it always aims to persuade) depends on the individual writer and subject. One inherent problem about travel writing is that the view is inevitably 'one-sided' (i.e. seen *only* through the eyes of the writer). How did local people (those fascinating natives, that traditional carpet-maker, these nomads or that woman pounding yams) actually *feel* about the intrusion of the writer into their world? As we read this extract, we are aware not only that our reading position is strictly British/European/Western (**context of immediate situation**), but also that any reading post-September 11th 2001 changes our position again (**context of cultural reference**). When Newby's book was published in 1958 it would have been read as a lively account of an amateurish and mildly eccentric expedition to a place few people knew anything about. The enthusiastic Introduction by the novelist Evelyn Waugh represents a typical contemporary response (**context of reception**). Remarking on the fondness for young Englishmen for 'wandering about the world for their amusement... to the great embarrassment of our officials', he relishes 'the understatement, the self-ridicule, the delight in the foreignness of foreigners,[and] the complete denial of any attempt to enlist the sympathies of his readers in the hardships he has capriciously invited'. Current knowledge of the complexities of the recent history of Afghanistan make this kind of light response impossible today.

ACTIVITY 60

Newby makes skilful use of point of view in this passage. In describing events (past and present), people and locations, how does Newby convey to the reader the *differing* perspectives of Hugh, Abdul Ghiyas and the narrative voice (i.e. Newby himself)?

Give examples to support your views.

Conclusion . . .

We conclude with a statement about context hammered out in the early stages of Curriculum 2000 by two English teacher-examiners, determined to 'pin down' this elusive concept once and for all . . .

> An examination of 'context' is an exploration and understanding of the ways in which the interpretation of a text changes through time. Readings of texts are affected by a variety of factors related both to their production by writers and their reception by readers. No reading can claim absolute authority, and texts cannot be outside the historical and cultural influences either of the time of their production or of the time of their reception, or of other texts.

In this book we have attempted to address all the issues raised in this statement, working with a methodology which allows us a flexible framework for contextual analysis, and which recognises the dynamic nature of 'woven' texts. As Jonathan Culler eloquently summarises: 'meaning is context-bound, but context is boundless'. Within the structure of our contextual frameworks, the possibilities for textual interpretations can be endlessly explored.